Groupwork Monographs

Groupwork Research

Other titles in the Groupwork Monographs Series

Groupwork Relationships (ISBN 9781861771056))

Structured Groupwork (9781861771063)

Groupwork with Older Adults (9781861771087)

Groupwork with Children and Families (9781861771094)

Groupwork and Social Action (9781861771100)

Groupwork and Mental Health (9781861771117)

Groupwork and Women (9781861771124)

Groupwork Monographs
Series Editor: Oded Manor

Groupwork Research

Edited by
Oded Manor

With an introduction by
Michael Preston-Shoot

W&B
MMIX

Published by Whiting & Birch Ltd,
Forest Hill, London SE23 3HZ

ISBN 9781861771070

Printed in England and the United States by Lightning Source

Groupwork Research

Contents

Preface

Each of the books in this series is an anthology of groupwork papers dedicated to one theme within the area of groupwork practice. The books can be used in a number of ways:

- *Practitioners* may draw on the ideas when considering their planned and current practice.
- *Students* may explore this pool of knowledge when expanding their understanding of groupwork.
- *Teachers and trainers* of groupwork may choose papers that direct their students to certain features of this method.
- *Researchers* may look for references that are still relevant to their particular area of study.

All will be invited to sample a pool of knowledge that has accumulated within the pages of the Journal *Groupwork* over almost two decades.

The series Groupwork Monographs is published by Whiting and Birch whose support of the Journal over the years has been vital. Ideas that had been initially raised in the editorial board of the journal led to these publications. We felt it would be good to offer readers a carefully selected collection of previously published papers. Papers that have withstood the test of time and can still meet current needs were sought. Indeed, re-publishing these papers is in itself a kind of message. We wanted to highlight the value of exciting groupwork knowledge and its relevance to current practice. In doing so, we wanted to encourage practitioners, students, teachers and researchers to enrich their practice through familiarity with this reservoir.

As the Series Editor, I reviewed all the papers published in *Groupwork* since its inception in 1988. This combing through previous publications was a very moving experience. Faces that I had known so well over so many years re-appeared and struggles in which I had participated came back to the surface. I felt privileged identifying appropriate papers and grouping these according to their themes. Sadly, some themes included too few papers to make a viable book. Of the viable themes some were well outside my direct experience and I asked various members of the editorial board of Groupwork to take responsibility for developing these into books.

Where my experiences as a practitioner, supervisor, researcher, teacher and editor in groupwork seemed fitting I undertook to form the actual books and invite specialists to write an introduction to each. I asked these specialists to comment on the contents of each paper, on the connections among the papers, and on the relevance of all to current practice and policies.

I think you will find these introductions very helpful – I certainly learnt something from reading each. I hope you will discover in each book something to go back to, so you can more easily go forward in developing, sustaining and enriching groupwork practice.

Oded Manor
Series Editor of Groupwork Monographs
London 2009

Notes from the Publisher

Approach to production

This volume comprises material published in *Groupwork* over several years. No textual amendments have been made, apart from the silent correction of a few spelling errors (that is, the *words* are exactly as originally published), and all but one of the chapters in this volume have been produced directly from the computer files of the original setting (the remaining chapter was produced from a scan of the original). Original heading levels and the like have also been retained. 'Keywords' have been added to earlier articles where not originally provided.

The *Groupwork* house style has been modified slightly over the years, and there will therefore be some inconsistency of referencing style between the chapters in this book.

Over the years, there have been changes in the typeface used for *Groupwork*, and we decided that rather than having a range of typographies in one book, all chapters should be recast in a single face (for those interested, Berkeley Oldstyle Book 10/12pt).

Citation

Authors citing material in this volume should recognise the original date and journal provenance as indicated by the house style of the publication for which they are writing, either by citing material as the original periodical article, or, if citing this volume, by clearly indicating the original date of publication of the material both in text references and in the bibliography. Assuming the house style of your publisher is based on Harvard, the reference list entry will look something like:

Home, A (1996) Enhancing research usefulness with adapted focus groups. *Groupwork*, 9, 2, 128-138 (Reprinted 2009, in O. Manor (Ed.) *Groupwork Research*, pp.82-92. London: Whiting & Birch)

The citation in the text will look something like: Home (1996/2009).

Author contact details

Authors' details are as at the date of publication. In case of difficulty in contacting any author refer to the publishers (enquiries@whitingbirch.net).

Introduction: Back to the future in groupwork research

Professor Michael Preston-Shoot

***Abstract**: The purpose of this introduction is to present the ten papers in this edited collection, relating them to one another and identifying within each core messages for groupwork practice. The chapter looks back in the sense of reviewing the themes that were prominent for writers at the time the papers were written. It also looks forward by signposting what further studies of groupwork research might be useful in the light of contemporary policy and practice concerns.*

The journal *Groupwork*, first published in 1988, has been a specialist reference source for practitioners and, arguably, the principal location within the United Kingdom for the development of groupwork theory, dissemination of groupwork research and evolution of groupwork practice. The ten papers that follow were all published originally in *Groupwork* and span fifteen years of the journal's output. They have as their core focus some aspect of groupwork research but, as the overview paper by Preston-Shoot (2004) demonstrates, they comprise less than a tenth of the journal's resource bank of empirical and conceptual articles. Some of the papers provide accounts of research methods in action (Birrell Weisen, 1991; Towl and Dexter, 1994; Harry et al., 1997-98). Some foreground the contribution of particular research methods to groupwork, such as focus groups (Home, 1996; Walton, 1996), community groups (Abu-Samah, 1996) and single system design (Johnson et al., 2001). Using groups is one way in which practitioners may be enabled to make sense of their practice (Smith, 1995). McDermott (2005), by contrast, fixes attention on the institutional location or affiliation of the groupwork researcher.

To a greater or lesser extent, each paper offers a review of groupwork research, an evaluation of particular methods and outcomes of groupwork practice, and signposts for further exploration. The papers, in one sense, offer evidence of what was preoccupying groupwork practitioners and analysts at the time they were written. They comprise, therefore, a historical record of the imperatives, dilemmas and concerns then pertaining. In another sense, individually and collectively, they provide the backdrop for a critical evaluation of groupwork research and a springboard for further theory building and evidence gathering. Much of the rest of this chapter will review this historical record by discussing the themes that cross-cut the papers. It will also pinpoint several themes that are becoming more prominent and will have to be factored into further work on methods of groupwork research.

Core messages

Preston-Shoot (2004) provides an overview of the status of groupwork research and evaluation in the UK. He suggests that both groupwork research and practice need to be strengthened if their contribution to service delivery is to be protected and advanced. What makes groups work, in practice and in education for practice, needs to be explored and understood more systematically. McDermott's paper (2005) picks up this argument and aims to fill in some of the gaps in research knowledge and methods. She addresses some of the complexities in researching groupwork and explores the contributions that particular research designs can make. It is a theory-based paper, leaving it to other writers to apply the ideas.

Smith's contribution (1995) is different. His focus is on enabling practitioners to manage their practice realities, in part through the contribution that groups can make to individual and organisational learning. He reports the findings of an evaluation of study groups and notes their ability to enhance people's learning as individuals and as a group. The paper, in common with some of the others, resonates with sound principles for effective practice, especially the importance of establishing and holding boundaries whilst working towards the gradual removal of barriers to dialogue.

Walton (1996) describes the use of focus groups and considers how issues of power and control can be addressed in research practice. She highlights the importance of stamina and courage, and of looking for commonalities between group members and between them and group facilitators, when seeking to practise and to enable empowerment. She foregrounds practice principles of role clarity, planning and support for groupworkers. Home (1996) also explores the use of focus groups as a method for bridging research and groupwork practice and skills. She illustrates the theory with an example and, in so doing, highlights the change that groupwork can evidence, including the advantages and disadvantages of the method.

Abu-Samah (1996) provides a detailed account of a qualitative research project. The theme of empowerment is again prominent. There is a consideration of the value of different research traditions. The paper gives an insight into the communities that were involved in the project and, in contrast to other papers, the voices of the participants are given space. Practice principles are also prominent, notably - building trust, respect, reciprocity and sharing. The paper provides evidence of how people can develop confidence to engage and to change.

The final four papers are also all accounts of groupwork research in action, the first an illustration of action research and the remainder examples of empirical studies. There is an evaluation of groupwork with offenders (Harry et al., 1997-98), which also describes how research was embedded in the culture of a probation service. Thus, the paper tracks the management of change to meet the demands of the evidence-based policy agenda as well as explores approaches to evaluation. The paper also evaluates the usefulness of different types of data, measures and techniques as evidence of individual change. Birrell Weisen (1991) researches the outcome of groupwork for people experiencing stress and anxiety. A number of groups are evaluated using standardised instruments and questionnaires to allow within and across group comparisons. Group content and research methods are described and evidence of change presented.

Towl and Dexter (1994) continue this theme. They evaluate anger management groupwork, similarly describing group content and research methods, when utilising principally standardised instruments. Once again, some significant change is reported together with an acknowledgement that mixed methods, including qualitative approaches, would have enhanced the findings and the understanding or interpretation of the results. Finally, Johnson et al. (2001) also take a research method, single system design, and illustrate through three examples its application. Using baseline and repeat measures, they show how to present evidence of change.

The latter papers in particular provide evidence of how groupwork can bring about change, sometimes using methods such as standardised instruments that are generally better known to psychologists than social workers and health care practitioners in the UK. They demonstrate the groupwork research literacy that can be learned and practised, and which the earlier papers call for in practice and in the education for professional practice.

Looking back

Several themes are prominent within and between the papers. They also have broader significance because of the emphasis within the modernisation agenda (DH, 1998) on evidence-based practice, accountability and outcomes.

Shifting practice context: The issue of accountability

The modernisation agenda has radically altered the context within which groupwork practice occurs. Preston-Shoot (2004) refers explicitly to this changing organisational and policy context, highlighting in particular the increasing emphasis on practitioners' accountability for the processes and outcomes of their work, and the priority now being given to evidence-based practice as an indicator of quality. Other writers, for example Macgowan (2006), have also linked the emergence of evidence-based groupwork practice to professional accountability. McDermott (2005) and Harry et al. (1997-98) also allude to the imperative to be evidence-based, the latter also demonstrating both how research enhances the added value to be gained from a culture of curiosity and how management support and ownership is vital. Johnson et al. (2001) also acknowledge the centrality of accountability, here framed as that of the practitioner to group member, group, agency and the public. Meanwhile, Smith (1995) shows the value of groupwork in enabling health and welfare professionals to manage their practice contexts.

It is worth noting that many of the papers within this volume were written and published before the modernisation agenda really took effect. However, it is debatable whether groupwork practice and research has fully engaged with and contested the trends in public services, including the impact of new public management on social work in particular and welfare provision more generally, other than to wonder where all the groupwork may have gone (Ward, 2002).

Practitioner-researcher: The convergence

Almost all the papers demonstrate explicitly or implicitly that practice skills parallel research skills and strongly advocate that practitioners should evaluate the processes and outcomes of their work. Interviewing, observing, planning, attending to process and to task, facilitating, analysing interactions and making assessments – these are research as well as practice skills (Home, 1996; Walton, 1996; McDermott, 2005).

For instance, Abu-Samah (1996) describes how techniques used to gain people's active involvement in groups were also groupwork-based research approaches. Their use and the information they discover and disseminate will enable individual practitioners and communities of interest to develop. Practice will become more meaningful because the information obtained will be useful not only for researchers but for group participants too (Abu-Samah, 1996). This reminds me of conferences which were planned as part of a research project on teaching, learning and assessing law in social work education (Braye and Preston-Shoot, 2005). Drawing on groupwork knowledge and skills, the events elicited information and interactions that enhanced the researchers' understanding of the issues and the participants' understanding of the impact of their perceptions and roles on others. Such participation and reflection is also embedded in the integration of research in practice described by Harry et al. (1997-98). Here too research is seen as modelling skills and values that are central to groupwork practice. Indeed, they advocate the demystification of groupwork and research as separate specialisms.

However, at least in social work, if not in other health and welfare professions, it remains unusual for practitioners to conduct research into practice. A similar picture emerges in education for professional practice. This is why the evidence base is limited in respect of the effectiveness of different methods of teaching, learning and assessment. Too often practitioners demonstrate ambivalent attitudes towards research and researchers, see practice and research skills as different, and doubt their competence to evaluate their work (Preston-Shoot, 2004). Macgowan (2006) makes similar observations, arguing that many practitioners have little incentive in their settings to generate evidence and that many organisations provide little support for evidence-based practice. As these papers demonstrate, a practitioner-researcher literature exists and groupwork provides an example of how a practice methodology can be evaluated. The challenge going forward is to embed this evaluative attitude of mind in all professional practice, including groupwork.

What counts as evidence?

The increasing focus on evidence-based practice raises two questions: what counts as evidence and whose evidence counts? Indeed, different stakeholders may well hold different perspectives on the value ascribed to particular sources of knowledge. McDermott (2005) acknowledges that this takes practitioners and researchers into contested terrain. She identifies issues of validity and reliability, trustworthiness and authenticity, and explores what different research designs, positivist and interpretivist, offer to researchers. Abu-Samah (1996) also explores debates and competing views concerning the contribution of quantitative and qualitative methods to the exploration of social reality.

Smith (1995) draws attention to how welfare professions have frequently imported knowledge without interrogating either its relevance or the traditions of actual practice. Indeed, the papers herein acknowledge rather than challenge head-on the value ascribed to different types of evidence. In this sense groupwork research has yet to fully realise the power of different types of knowledge, namely the reported experience of groupwork members, policy and practice literature, and empirical accounts (Pawson et al., 2003). It has only begun to engage in debate about whether there is, or should be a hierarchy of best evidence, as proposed by Macgowan (2006), or whether the challenge is, or should be to triangulate different sources of evidence and knowledge, as proposed by Pawson et al. (2003). It has also yet to exploit fully approaches designed to evidence different outcomes (Carpenter, 2005), namely people's reactions, attitude change, knowledge and skill acquisition, behaviour change, and organisational change. Macgowan (2006) articulates this point most clearly. Evidence must be rigorous and relevant, with the consequence that practitioners, whether or not also researchers, must be able to distinguish between different types of evidence and to access tools to examine the evidence available.

The nature of outcomes

Both in children's services and adult services, government social policy now identifies the outcomes to which provision must aspire and contribute, whether for children in need, children requiring protection, or adults needing care and services. Unsurprisingly, then, the papers in this volume consider the relationship between research and outcomes, a concern with efficacy which Macgowan (2006) also evidences when summarising the findings of some systematic reviews of particular forms of groupwork and advocating the use of standardised instruments to assess the impact of particular intra-group and extra-group factors. Preston-Shoot (2004) identifies the challenge of demonstrating a link between groupwork practice and outcomes. He acknowledges practitioners' need to show success as well as their distrust of the focus on outcomes. He points out methodological opportunities and options for seeking to understand and explain what happens in groups. McDermott (2005) addresses one such challenge, namely the imperative to research not just what is easily researchable but what is important for different stakeholders. Along with Walton (1996) and Johnson et al. (2001), she too stresses the importance of evaluating processes as well as outcomes. Carpenter's work (2005), referred to above, is helpful in enabling practitioners and researchers to think through what they want to find out and the different methods that then open out.

Research methods and techniques figure in several papers. The initial task of aligning research methods to the research question is stressed by Preston-Shoot (2004) and McDermott (2005). The importance of taking baseline measures is covered by McDermott (2005) as well as Towl and Dexter (1994). Walton (1996) highlights the importance of support for groupworkers whilst preparation emerges as key through all the contributions. Different approaches to demonstrating outcomes are discussed in several papers (Birrell Weisen, 1991; Towl and Dexter, 1994; Abu-Samah, 1996; Harry et al., 1997-98; Johnson et al., 2001). In the main these papers provide evidence of the value and results of a particular method of gathering and analysing data. Together with Smith (1995), they illustrate how group members can engage in reflection and learning, including when confronted with personally sensitive or challenging material. They offer evidence for the effectiveness of groupwork in addressing a variety of situations, including anxiety and stress, bereavement, resettlement, offending, and anger management.

The value of groupwork

The value of groupwork will only be appreciated if research findings are disseminated. Both Home (1996) and Harry et al. (1997-98) devote some space to this important but often neglected task within groupwork and research, emphasising approaches which aim to ensure an impact on policy and practice. In addition, both McDermott (2005) and Smith (1995) identify ways in which groupwork can address issues of equality, whilst Preston-Shoot (2004) and Home (1996) draw attention to some of the advantages as well as some of the drawbacks of groupwork as a method of intervention. Throughout, however, even if the word "empowerment" is not used specifically, the papers convey a real sense of the difference that groupwork can make to individual members, to groups and to the organisational context within which they are located.

Signposts forward

Reading again the papers for this volume, several issues or questions appear rather marginalised. Given contemporary social policy preoccupations with accountability, safeguarding and quality (DH, 1998) and, at least for adults requiring care or services, with personalisation and inclusion, groupwork practice and research will, arguably, have to give greater prominence to at least five themes.

Involvement

In his overview of groupwork research, Preston-Shoot (2004) questions why experts by experience (usually called 'users') are not more visible as either contributors to groupwork's bibliography or as voices in practice accounts reported by practitioners. McDermott (2005) similarly notes the apparent omission of the involvement of groupwork participants in measuring outcomes or effectiveness, which may be significant when considered in the light of different stakeholders holding diverse perspectives on evaluation. She also comments that group members as well as leaders or facilitators may act as researchers, either formally or in the sense of researching themselves. Both conclude that greater emphasis is needed on how group members perceive the value and effectiveness of groupwork interventions.

Walton (1996), Abu-Samah (1996), and Harry et al. (1997-98) also touch upon partnership. Walton refers to a greater sharing of power with service users. Abu-Samah's practice is based on an explicit principle of active involvement and commitment to empowerment, with active dialogue producing benefits for, and shifts in the thinking of both researcher and participants. This shift in understanding has also been noted elsewhere in a context of using groups to bring diverse stakeholders together to inform research and policy-making (Braye and Preston-Shoot, 2005). Harry et al. (1997-98) also involved group members in producing evaluations from their own perspective and describe how those being supervised by probation officers were included in the development of groupwork programmes.

Partnership in groupwork practice and in research, or what Abu-Samah calls 'subject to subject relationships', was particularly foregrounded by Mullender and Ward (1991) in their work on self-directed groupwork. Here groupworkers were facilitators, assisting group members to use their power and authority to engage with issues of relevance to them. It is hard to escape the conclusion, however, that groupwork planning, practice and dissemination may not have kept pace with how partnership and empowerment practice has been developed elsewhere. Contemporary policy concern with personalisation of service provision adds further urgency to this imperative.

Insider-researchers

Whether it is groupworkers and/or group participants who are researching their experience, they are evaluating something of which they are a part. In that sense they are insider-researchers. However, this too is an under-theorised and under-reported issue. For example, although both Home (1996) and Harry et al. (1997-98) advocate that practitioner-researchers should be reflectively critical of their groupwork activity, neither discusses the advantages and challenges of bringing an analytical lens to focus on one's own practice.

McDermott's paper alone (2005) focuses explicitly on this particular issue. She recognises that an insider position can both enrich perspective but also obscure understanding of processes and outcomes. She advocates that insider-researchers should acknowledge the limits and advantages of their location, and use supervision and recording to enable them to step back from the action in order to focus more reflectively and critically on what may be happening. Walton (1996) also refers to the importance of practitioners bringing a research lens to inform their own practice and to critique agency policies. She comments on the importance of having an ability to be involved in a system whilst also being able to stand back and focus in upon aims and processes. Johnson et al. (2001) also refer to insider research, partly in the context of accountability to group members, agencies and the wider public. They register interest in practitioners conducting research on their own practice and suggest that one advantage will prove to reside in the issues selected for research being of significant concern to the groupworker. However, as elsewhere, such a location is seen as relatively unproblematic.

It is surprising, therefore, how little engagement there has been with insider issues, both in groupwork and more generally in the research literature. Campbell (1997) argues that the convergence of practice and research in agency settings poses dilemmas for practitioner-researchers. She articulates a number of unintended consequences that can emerge particularly through insider-research, including the impact that loyalty and gratitude, concerns about continued access to services, and personal investment may have on data collection and analysis, use of the information collected, and subsequent relationships. A personal and/or agency need for success has been noted elsewhere (O'Connor, 1992). She explores issues surrounding confidentiality, rights to participate and withdraw, informed consent, and the relationship of research to the practice process which, whilst present for outsider-researchers as well as insider-researchers, are particularly significant for the latter.

Other writers, too, have focused on aspects of insider research (Zeni, 1998; Kanuha, 2000; Coy, 2006), recognising that this location brings both opportunities and challenges. The issues with which they engage include:

- Negotiating access within an agency, including acknowledging any demand for good news and keeping safe the space to be critical;
- Negotiating access with participants, including ensuring rights to participate and withdraw;
- Demonstrating trust and care with relationships, including when participants might need support, whether particular data can be used, how contributions might be acknowledged but anonymity and confidentiality preserved when requested, and how writing up and dissemination are managed;
- Balancing the roles of researcher and practitioner;
- Reflecting on the impact on the researcher role of prior and ongoing relationships, and of power and authority on what data is offered;
- Reflecting on the impact on the practitioner role of working together on research and of the personal need for evidence of success.

These writers suggest the use of critical friends, supervision, triangulation of data, and access to ethical guidance as ways of realising the opportunities and navigating through the challenges of insider-research.

Nonetheless, outsider-researcher is the dominant model in groupwork and other research literature. This has important repercussions for consideration of ethics and training. Equally, the dominant assumption is that the organisational environment is benign, supportive of practitioner-research. However, this assumption cannot be relied upon and both outsider-researchers and insider-researchers may well confront organisational dynamics that challenge the very basis of ethical and knowledge-informed research practice (Preston-Shoot et al., 2008).

Ethics

Research governance has become increasingly prominent in social work and social care. This change has been introduced in the United Kingdom because other professions, such as psychology and health care, had given far more attention to research ethics. In groupwork, Campbell (1997) has suggested that ethical codes provide insufficient depth and specificity for groupwork researchers, juxtaposing this with what she suggests is the ethical minefield of agency-based research. A review of papers in this volume, and in the groupwork literature more generally, finds little attention paid to ethical approval of research and subsequent monitoring of projects.

McDermott (2005) explicitly focuses on ethical considerations, such as consent to participation and non-intrusive methods, but the attention given is somewhat cursory. Walton (1996) refers to the ethical responsibility to disseminate the findings of her research and to ensure their influence on service development, in acknowledgement of the aims of those who participated in her focus group. She also stresses the centrality of values to practice and identifies the centrality of power and control issues to planning and undertaking research and groupwork. However, the paper gives little detail about how values and research ethics were assured. Home (1996) also refers to ethics as a planning issue but, likewise, gives no detailed consideration. The remainder of the papers are silent on how ethical issues were addressed in groupwork planning and practice even though several refer to goals of empowerment.

Preston-Shoot et al. (2008) provide an illustration of just what Campbell (1997) refers to, namely - intra and inter-agency politics and dynamics which can threaten the ethical basis of research. They also offer an analysis of the mechanisms that might help groupworkers to consider ethical issues not only during the planning process but subsequently. In a policy climate where accountability and quality are prominent concerns, and in an organisational environment where judicial reviews, inquiries and Ombudsman reports uncover unlawful, unethical and/or unsafe practice (Braye and Preston-Shoot, 2009), there is surely scope for greater consideration of what groupwork knowledge can contribute to research governance decision-making.

Education for groupwork and research

Preston-Shoot (2004) refers to groupwork education as being variable. He also suggests that guidance in the literature for groupwork research is variable, which leaves practitioners uncertain about their skills and about which methods to adopt (Home, 1996; McDermott, 2005). As Johnson et al. (2001) acknowledge, teaching research methods has been part of accreditation standards in the United States, requiring students to be skilled both as consumers of research and in evaluating their own practice. Macgowan (2006), also writing from a US context, suggests that education for groupwork should include the value of evidence-based groupwork, the selection of best evidence, the evidence base of different groupwork theories, the relationship between different groupwork components and outcomes, and research instruments. He also reminds readers of the importance of ongoing training and consultation and advocates the development of collaborative practitioner-researcher networks. In a UK context, networks such as *Making Research Count* and organisations such as the *Social Care Institute for Excellence* could be vehicles for disseminating groupwork research methods and findings.

Groupwork and research knowledge and skills are highlighted in the social work benchmark statement (QAA, 2008), and both small groups and research evidence feature prominently in the content and delivery of professional education. Nevertheless, questions remain about the degree to which groupwork itself is taught in social work education and practised in health and welfare agencies. Moreover, notwithstanding the increased focus in government policy on evidence, groupwork texts continue to give little space to research and evaluation. At the same time, practitioners and managers remain ambivalent about the interface between research and organisational practice. Finally, the evidence base underpinning the teaching, learning and assessment of groupwork practice and of research in professional qualifying programmes has not been systematically reviewed.

Conclusion

Whether working in an inter-agency and/or inter-disciplinary context, or as a groupworker in an agency employing particular professionals for particular roles and tasks, a key task is making one's knowledge explicit. Harry et al. (1997-98) identify this responsibility explicitly but all the papers may be read in just this way. All bring to a wider audience the knowledge, values and skills that informed and were evidenced by groupwork practice and research. By looking back at these papers now, we can move forward armed with a rich source of material for beginning and experienced groupworkers alike, and a reservoir of ideas for those intent on researching policy and practice. As this introduction has made clear, that is a professional responsibility. Indeed it is one which has a greater degree of urgency now, given the searching spotlight that is being shone by policy-makers on the outcomes of service provision and of professional education for practice.

References

Abu-Samah, A. (1996) 'Empowering research process: using groups in research to empower the people', *Groupwork*, 9 (2), 221-252.

Birrell Weisen, R. (1991) 'Evaluative study of groupwork for stress and anxiety', *Groupwork*, 4 (2), 152-162.

Braye, S. and Preston-Shoot, M. (2005) 'Emerging from out of the shadows? Service user and carer involvement in systematic reviews', *Evidence and Policy*, 1 (2), 173-193.

Braye, S. and Preston-Shoot, M. (2009) *Practising Social Work Law (3rd ed).* Basingstoke: Palgrave Macmillan.

Campbell, L. (1997) 'Good and proper: considering ethics in practice research', *Australian Social Work*, 50 (4), 29-36.

Carpenter, J. (2005) *Evaluating Outcomes in Social Work Education.* London and Dundee: Social Care Institute for Excellence and Scottish Institute for Excellence in Social Work Education.

Coy, M. (2006) 'This morning I'm a researcher: this afternoon I'm an outreach worker: ethical dilemmas in practitioner research', *International Journal of Social Research Methodology*, 9 (5), 419-431.

Department of Health (1998) *Modernising Social Services.* London: The Stationery Office.

Harry, R., Heggarty, P., Lisles, C., Thurston, R. and Vanstone, M. (1997-98) 'Research into practice does go: integrating research within programme development', *Groupwork*, 10 (2), 107-125.

Home, A. (1996) 'Enhancing research usefulness with adapted focus groups', *Groupwork*, 9 (2), 128-138.

Johnson, P., Beckerman, A. and Auerbach, C. (2001) 'Researching our own practice: single system design for groupwork', *Groupwork*, 13 (1), 57-72.

Kanuha, V. (2000) 'Being native versus going native: conducting social work research as an insider', *Social Work*, 45 (5), 439-447.

Macgowan, M. (2006) 'Evidence-based group work: a framework for advancing best practice', *Journal of Evidence-Based Social Work*, 3 (1), 1-21.

McDermott, F. (2005) 'Researching groupwork: outsider and insider perspectives', *Groupwork*, 15 (1), 90-108.

Mullender, A. and Ward, D. (1991) *Self-Directed Groupwork: Users Take Action for Empowerment*. London: Whiting and Birch.

O'Connor, I. (1992) 'Bereaved by suicide: setting up an "ideal" therapy group in the real world', *Groupwork*, 5 (3), 74-86.

Pawson, R., Boaz, A., Grayson, L., Long, A. and Barnes, C. (2003) *Types and Quality of Knowledge in Social Care*. London: Social Care Institute for Excellence.

Preston-Shoot, M. (2004) 'Evidence: the final frontier? Star Trek, groupwork and the mission of change', *Groupwork*, 14 (3), 18-43.

Preston-Shoot, M., Wigley, V., McMurray, I. and Connolly, H. (2008) 'Reflections on ethical research in action: working at the practice edge', *Ethics and Social Welfare*, 2 (2), 150-171.

QAA (2008) *Subject Benchmark Statements: Social Work*. Gloucester: The Quality Assurance Agency for Higher Education.

Smith, M. (1995) 'Developing critical conversations about practice', *Groupwork*, 8 (2), 134-151.

Towl, G. and Dexter, P. (1994) 'Anger management groupwork with prisoners: an empirical evaluation', *Groupwork*, 7 (3), 256-269.

Walton, P. (1996) 'Focus groups and familiar social work skills: their contribution to practitioner research', *Groupwork*, 9 (2), 139-153.

Ward, D. (2002) 'Groupwork', in R. Adams, L. Dominelli and M. Payne (eds) *Social Work: Themes, Issues and Critical Debates (2nd ed)*. Basingstoke: Palgrave Macmillan.

Zeni, J. (1998) 'A guide to ethical issues and action research', *Educational Action Research*, 6 (1), 9-19.

Michael Preston-Shoot is Professor of Social Work and Dean of the Faculty of Health and Social Sciences, University of Bedfordshire, Luton, England.

Evidence: The final frontier? Star Trek, groupwork and the mission of change

Michael Preston-Shoot

Abstract: *This paper uses the Star Trek metaphor to explore research and evaluation in groupwork practice in the United Kingdom. It begins this exploration within the modernisation agenda and then surveys the practice of evidencing groupwork as disseminated through one specialist journal (A summary of each of the 17 papers considered is given in the appendix.). It offers suggestions for strengthening evaluation, and groupwork's position within modernised services, by researching more systematically what makes groups work.*

Keywords: *evidence, evaluation, research, systematic review, groupwork practice.*

Trailer

Captain's Log, Star Date late 2004. The Star Ship Groupwork is locked in orbit around Planet Evaluation. The crew appears uncertain about beaming down to engage with the life forms on this planet, a significant part of the modernisation solar system. The mission, however, is to survey evaluation in groupwork practice and to strengthen the evidencing of groupwork. The search is for knowledge crystals that will support the crew in engaging with metanoia, a shift of mind towards researching more systematically what makes groups work.

Star Fleet Command

Star Fleet Command is modernising the galaxy over which it presides (Department of Health, 1998). Key benchmarks for social work and health related services, and for probation and youth justice practice, are that provision should be characterised by:

- Standards and accountability, to ensure role clarity, consistent quality and the protection of service users from ineffective and abusive practice
- Responsiveness and flexibility, to ensure that the needs of service users rather than the imperatives of providers are paramount
- Inclusion and involvement, to ensure that user and carer perspectives shape service design, planning, development and evaluation.

One further benchmark, and the focus of this article, is that services should be evidence-based. In terms of groupwork planning, delivery and evaluation, this suggests a focus on what value the intervention adds. Indeed, Pollio (2002) identifies accountability as a prominent theme in the United States and suggests that the failure to incorporate evidence into practice is an ethical violation.

For the crew of the Star Ship Groupwork, modernisation is an externally driven mission of change but there is, as yet, little published evidence of how groupworkers are adjusting to this new world. In fact, the mission of delivering evidence-based groupwork might be challenging. Some writers have conceded that their approach to assessing effectiveness has been insufficiently rigorous or systematic (Cowburn, 1990; Mulvie, 1991). It is arguable too that evaluative research on outcomes of groupwork practice and groupwork's conceptual base is scarce, making it difficult for instance to advance groupwork as the intervention of choice or to distinguish between the merits of smaller or larger, open or closed groups.

Discovering new galaxies: Working with Klingons and Romulans

Star Fleet Command has for some time been reaching out towards other galaxies, such as the independent and voluntary sectors, seeing their occupants as perhaps more suited to the task of providing some services. Increasingly too Star Fleet Command envisages new organisational forms for the delivery of services, with old galactic divisions between social work and health, housing or education being abandoned in favour of inter-professional and multidisciplinary partnerships in single Star Ships. New professional qualifications and new skill mixes will emerge, for instance for youth justice and for Connexions workers. This will require the crew of Star Ship Groupwork to voyage around new galaxies and to work with life forms previously regarded as alien or hostile.

Captain's log

Leading the Star Ship Groupwork is a significantly different enterprise now. The Care Standards Act 2000 requires that crew members engage in continuing professional development in order to maintain their membership of the workforce. The Public Interest Disclosure Act 1998 empowers the crew of Star Ship Groupwork to speak out against unlawful or unethical practice. The Human Rights Act 1998 requires the crew to ensure that their groupwork practice does not amount to inhuman and degrading treatment, and they must act proportionately when restricting anyone's enjoyment of family life, confidentiality, faith, personal expression and liberty. The Act has given added force to the principle of not discriminating against particular life forms encountered in known or newly discovered galaxies. Indeed, the life forms that the crew encounters can now expect to be included as partners in mapping the needs and setting the standards to which the service must respond, in working towards mutually agreed goals, and in monitoring and evaluating the outcomes achieved.

These changes to the mission of Star Ship Groupwork are, however, welcome since they support rather than undermine the principle of empowerment that underpins the accepted mission of individual change and social justice (IASSW, 2001) and the knowledge of what service users find facilitative in their encounters with the crew. There is little published evidence, however, which indicates groupwork's current location in respect of these developments.

A final frontier?

There have been questions asked about whether the Star Ship Groupwork can survive in a work environment where procedural practice and managerialism dominate, and in a policy context that dehumanises groups as diverse as young people, asylum seekers and adults with severe mental distress. Its mission to establish colonies on particular planets has met with variable success, for example in probation where different observers have reported it to be both well established but also outside mainstream practice (Caddick, 1991; Senior, 1991). Indeed, Ward (2002) asks where groupwork has gone. Even where there have been champions and a staff development focus, groupwork has remained a minority method within the workforce (Doel and Sawdon, 1999).

Yet groupwork is a method of choice with a range of client groups and issues (Heap, 1992; Pollio, 2002). In part this is because of the capacity of even the most troubled individuals to make use of it (Ward, 1995). In part it is because groupwork can engage people at different levels (Mullender, 1996) - intrapersonal, interpersonal, socio-psychological and socio-structural. In part it is because it addresses themes at the leading edge of professional activity - powerlessness and hopelessness, guilt and shame, denial and resistance, acceptance and support (Shulman, 1988).

The mission

Locating the evidence of groupwork's value and relevance must, then, be part of the mission in order to capture the space opened up by the social policy concern with best value. Powerful claims are indeed advanced for groupwork's potential to realise individual and social change. On balance the evidence for individual change appears stronger than that for social change, perhaps because of the traditional focus of much professional activity. Both self-help groups and worker facilitated groups report changes in how people perceive experiences and issues, how they feel, how they speak about and resolve issues, and how they engage with others (see, for example, Hopmeyer and Werk, 1993; Garrett, 1995; Hill, 2001). However, De Lois (2003), Mullender and Ward (1991), and Ni Chorcora et al (1994) demonstrate that it is possible to use groupwork to promote partnership and dialogue and to effect structural change.

In this quest, despite numerous practitioner evaluations of groupwork's effectiveness, the current state of the research evidence appears variable in terms of demonstrating that groupwork planning, delivery and outcomes are appropriate and relevant, acceptable and equitable, effective and efficient. Concern lingers (Matzat, 1993; Hopmeyer and Werk, 1993) of a lack of research and of comparative studies without which it remains difficult to maximise the beneficial aspects of groupwork and to collect data for theory building and refinement. So how might the engine of the Star Ship Groupwork get the crew to warp speed?

Engine room

There are five crystals - knowledge drivers - in the engine room (Pawson et al, 2003). The first is the reported experience of service users and carers. This knowledge driver is not delivering its full power. It is an untapped resource when seeking to identify what works, what is of value. A review of published papers in this journal, *Groupwork*, will not find any written exclusively by group members, even amongst the articles that explore the outcomes of self-help groups. There are only two where service users appear as co-contributors (Ni Chorcora et al, 1994; Wintram et al, 1994). Articles written by groupworkers do sometimes report the views of group members, but not always in their own words (see, for example, Rhule, 1988). One criterion for future assessment of submitted papers, which describe and evaluate practice, might be the degree to which they give voice to group members.

A second driver is the policy literature - reviews, inspections and inquiries. This too is not delivering full power, perhaps because standards have yet to be developed in the United Kingdom, unlike the United States (AASWG, 1999), for groupwork practice. The conceptual base is surely sufficiently well developed to enable standards to be articulated against which practice can be reviewed.

The third driver comprises perspectives from students and practitioners. Practice generated knowledge is available but, as the next section will demonstrate, it is unbalanced for the task of responding to the quality agenda set by Star Fleet Command. The same applies to the fourth driver, namely groupwork research in the form of empirical and theoretical accounts, both of practice outcomes but also of evaluation methodologies. It also appears to be true that what research informed knowledge is available is under-utilised by groupworkers.

The fifth driver is education for groupwork practice. Again, a subsequent section will explore this driver in more detail. However, this driver is also not delivering full power through taught academic and practice curricula.

Different sections of the crew of the Star Ship Groupwork may be found amongst the contributors to the knowledge base but one potential dilithium crystal, or resource, which is not fully exploited is cross-level generated knowledge. Different sections of the crew could work together more regularly to make sense of their lived experiences of work. Similarly, the imperative to engage with Klingons and Romulans, has meant that published work is available from other galaxies but, judging from the pages of *Groupwork*, there is little evidence yet of inter-professional or multidisciplinary generated knowledge. Getting to warp speed, however, is not just a matter of exploiting the power of each of these crystals. It is also a matter of triangulating these data sources in order to generate the most power from the conceptual base, the map of the stars that exists.

Getting to warp speed

For this paper the author reviewed articles published in *Groupwork* between 1988 and 2003 and identified only five with a central focus on evaluation and research. Preston-Shoot (1988) argues that for groupwork to secure a place among methods, evaluation must become an essential feature of practice. His paper outlines the importance of adopting a consciously evaluative approach to groupwork practice and presents a model for evaluating process and outcomes. Peake and Otway (1990) similarly argue that groupwork should be evaluated. For them, one measure of success could be attendance levels, linked to the group's curriculum, rules, selection of members and choice of groupworkers.

Gordon (1992) suggests that, when practice improvement is the aim of evaluation, an illuminative paradigm will provide more valuable information than the traditional experimentalist research paradigm. In the latter a sequence is followed that begins with itemising aims and objectives and continues with generating pre-group measures that can be repeated once groupwork concludes. Conclusions are then drawn from the analysed data. The illuminative paradigm proceeds with a variety of techniques in order to develop an understanding of a group through a process of observation, inquiry, dialogue and explanation.

Harry and colleagues (1997-98) provide an account of a continuous process of evaluation. They advocate a realist approach to evaluation, based on a self-reflexive learning model. A range of methods, sources and times is used, with emphasis on encouraging ownership of evaluation and integrating findings into practice. Finally, Johnson and colleagues (2001) suggest that single system design is a particularly suitable method of monitoring groupwork practice. They demonstrate how it is possible to use a baseline period as a time for exploration, followed by an intervention period when groupworkers intervene intentionally in group process to effect change.

The research driver in the engine room appears under-resourced for releasing the power of evaluation methodologies. For this paper the author also reviewed a sample of recent books published in the United Kingdom and found a similar picture. Douglas (2000) does not refer to research or evaluation but in an earlier text (1991) he warns of starting to evaluate practice too late, that is not at the point of departure. He acknowledges that it can be difficult to assess the quantity and quality of change and to be sure that it is the result of groupwork. He therefore emphasises the importance of well-established baselines and the use of instruments to measure change. Phillips (2001) locates evaluation as part of quality assurance and links it with the setting of clear goals, which provide the framework for subsequent assessment of effectiveness. Observation, feedback sheets and follow up are amongst the methods recommended.

Barnes and colleagues (1999) devote less than a page to the importance of groupworkers having a research orientation in order to retain curiosity about theory and practice. Doel and Sawdon (1999) write more expansively about evaluation while denying themselves the space to detail how research methodology might apply to groups. They identify a range of action techniques alongside group discussion, empirical measures, and written evaluations. In similar vein, Whitaker (2001) urges groupworkers to monitor and assess groups in order to be self-critical, to inform practice and to articulate beneficial outcomes. She also lists some approaches to evaluation, including post session reviews and periodic formal reviews. Once again, however, if there are blocks to releasing the energy for evaluation, more could have been offered that might enable groupworkers and members alike to explore similar and divergent views about content and process, which would enable them to account to others, to develop the knowledge base, to inform practice and to locate success.

A further review of articles published in the first thirteen volumes of *Groupwork* reveals additional interesting findings. For this purpose a threefold division was used, namely:

- Conceptual and theory building papers, where the contributor's purpose is to develop or review ideas about some aspect of groupwork
- Descriptive papers, where the contributor's main focus is to describe a group but where some evaluation may be included
- Empirical papers, where the contributor's focus is to research into groupwork processes and/or outcomes from the perspectives of the different people involved.

Using these criteria for selection, 111 papers were assessed as focusing primarily on research as theory building and conceptual development. They were designed to develop and/or illustrate part of groupwork's methodology. 104 papers were assessed as principally describing groupwork in practice. Sometimes, usually at a single end point, they contained an evaluation from the groupworkers' and/or members' perspective of what benefits or learning were derived from this experience. Only 17 papers were categorised as empirical evaluations (see appendix).

The purpose here is not to privilege one type of paper, nor indeed one approach to evaluation. It is to identify how groupworkers may be limiting their horizons by failing to make use of a range of structured approaches to data collection and evaluation.

Beam me up

The prospect of being transported to Planet Evaluation emerges through the literature as a voyage into a world of craters, inhospitable atmospheres and uncharted, barren terrain. It is not surprising, then, that the literature offers more by way of descriptive and conceptual accounts than research-based evidence.

Some groupworkers appear quite uncertain about how to review their practice. Clarke and Aimable (1990) did not undertake any formal evaluation of their group with members, recognising that they had underestimated members' ability. They do not appear to have considered what other methods may have been employed to evaluate inputs or outcomes. Tribe and Shackman (1989) recorded that they only felt able to judge the usefulness of the group by the fact that members kept attending and talking of its value. These measures are valuable as sources of evidence but others might have been utilised to explore the sense of community and support that members said they gained. One explanation for the uncertainty might be the limited focus in the groupwork literature on evaluation methods.

Another might revolve around training in research and evaluation, both generally and in respect of groupwork. Manor (2003) suggests that groupworkers need to be consciously trained in systematic evaluation. It is arguable that training in research and evaluation methods has been squeezed in the curriculum hitherto in social work education. Similarly squeezed has been groupwork itself, with students reporting that they spend much of their time working with or in groups but feel inadequately prepared for the task (Reid, 1988; Marsh and Triseliotis, 1996; Mathias-Williams and Thomas, 2002). A vicious circular orbit emerges: the less training practitioners receive, the less groupwork is practised, the less training is identified as being required. Or, alternatively, the less training is given, the more practitioners doubt their competence to work with groups, the less groupwork is practised and researched, and so on. Nor does this appear to be a uniquely United Kingdom phenomenon (Habermann, 1993; Kurland and Salmon, 1993).

Star Fleet Command has issued new occupational standards for social work (TOPSS, 2002) and subject benchmark statement (QAA, 2000). Both require that practitioners are prepared for and capable of working in and with groups, which includes knowledge and skills for reviewing and evaluating the outcomes of such practice. Both clearly link assessment, planning, goal setting and evaluation. Professional competence clearly includes the ability to provide evidence for judgements and to monitor effectiveness in meeting need (TOPSS, 2002). It includes using research concepts and tools from social work and other disciplines to understand groups, guide action, support critical reflection and use a range of approaches in evaluating practice outcomes (QAA, 2000). It remains to be seen how these educational changes will be reflected in research and evaluation academic and practice curricula and, subsequently in the groupwork literature.

Perhaps, however, deflecting shields are being used. O'Connor (1992) has hypothesised that practitioners might have an innate need to demonstrate success. This leads her to argue the need for honesty in evaluation, prioritising critical appraisal through the use of recording and supervision. The theme of defensive evaluation practice appears elsewhere too (Barnes et al, 1999). Having to prove value and effectiveness to those who may be sceptical might lead to a choice of methods most likely to generate good news.

Indeed, it is possible to see the lack of attention to follow-up data in this light. Pennells (1995) noticed that member progress from one group was not sustained after the group concluded. Indeed, it fell to levels below those measured on initial referral. Evaluation may challenge cherished theory. In this instance, the commitment to time limited groupwork may have resulted in insufficient emphasis being given to consolidation and to working through. Learning and change may decay over time, and it would seem pertinent to explore what factors within groups and post groups enable retention of newly acquired knowledge, skills and attitudes.

Deflecting shields of a different type may be present in comments concerning difficulties within evaluation. Thus, there is the difficulty of being certain that outcomes are related to the groupwork intervention rather than intervening variables (Johnson et al, 2001). Towl and Dexter (1994) acknowledge the problem of defining and measuring change but move the debate on by identifying a range of tools and by suggesting that data from these be triangulated to overcome the limitations of each technique. The tools include observation, reports, behavioural checklists and questionnaires. Gordon (1992) identifies several reservations about traditional experimentalist research designs. These include ethical issues surrounding use of control groups, oversimplification of goals and insufficient flexibility to incorporate newly emerging needs.

However, some crew members of Star Ship Groupwork might want to set their phasers on 'stun' since they are concerned with the very focus on outcomes. Sometimes this derives from the nature of the group envisaged. Thus, Schneewind (1996) states that a concern with formal evaluation discourages reports of groups that do not have a planned termination date and where membership is self-selected. Maggs-Rapport (2000) writes that it is difficult to conceive outcomes when a project evolves through dialogue with members. Gordon (1992) advocates an illuminative evaluation paradigm for similar reasons, stressing how groups contain multiple realities and how participants influence each other. Rather than outcomes it is evolving processes that should be explored through observation, recording, and dialogue. Yet, Schneewind (1996) seems concerned with quantitative analysis. It should be possible to align evaluative design with a group's structure and to express aims and objectives as outcomes that can then be researched. For example, Otway and Peake (1994) describe a needs-led approach to work with women whose children had been sexually abused. This was an open, open-ended group, where members set the agenda and assessed personal change in terms of the behavioural challenges presented by their children and the stress levels that they experienced as parents.

Sometimes the concern is with outcomes *per se*. Brown (1996) is critical of the obsession with outcomes because it may lead to a neglect of process and indeed assume that outcomes can be defined. The commitment to improved outcomes for services requires agreement on what outcomes are sought and on how effectiveness is to be understood. Yet what is competent and effective practice is a contested concept (Preston-Shoot, 2004). Service users and carers value in professional intervention the quality of relationships and interpersonal and practice skills (Barnes, 2002). Managers, however, appear to prioritise procedural and instrumental skills, knowledge of the law and procedures, whilst practitioners emphasise process and interpersonal skills, and knowledge from empirical research and of methods of intervention (Marsh and Triseliotis, 1996).

Such reservations about outcomes also connect with anxieties more generally about the quality strategy within the modernisation agenda, namely that it evaluates only what is easily measurable. They may connect too with scepticism that political and managerial commitment does not exist to alter policy or practice in line with evaluation findings (Humphreys et al, 2003).

'It's groupwork, Michael, but not as we know it'

The Star Ship Groupwork, very much in common with its sister ships, has not embraced the idea of the practitioner researcher. Practice has not been defined as a research site, although Whitaker and Archer (1994) suggest that research and practice are comparable and have described one approach whereby researchers, practitioners and managers can engage in producing substantive findings that extend knowledge and understanding. In suggesting that groupworkers adopt a more consciously evaluative approach to their practice, the challenge is to transport groupwork to a different position. It is to engage fully with evaluated groupwork as a life form. The justification for such a shift is that an essential element of a groupworker's activity is the obligation to appraise their effectiveness. It is difficult otherwise to conceive how groupworkers can comment authoritatively about the needs they encounter, about the impact or effectiveness of social policies, and about the empowering aspects of their practice, without an evidenced practice base. Nor will they be able to challenge how others might construct evidence or seek to marginalise service user and carer narratives. Thus, the justification is to bring a different and empirically supported perspective to needs and problem analysis, to theory and to practice (Kolbo et al, 1997/98; Whitaker, 2001).

The literature conveys an impression of difficulty in connecting with what evaluation methodology may have to offer. Pennells (1995), in the context of work with bereaved children, writes of the struggle to evaluate effectively and yet uses meetings with families and referrers, questionnaires for children, and group member self-evaluation. Perhaps the problem is not knowing what tools are available and the challenge demystifying what can count as effective evidence.

Searching the frequencies

A systematic review of the research and evaluation literature will provide groupworkers with information about the range of methodologies available. A systematic review of the groupwork literature will provide them with possible outcome criteria (see, for example, Otway and Peake, 1994) and knowledge for practice. Indeed, Pollio (2002) suggests that the evidence-based groupworker should review prior findings when deciding what is current best practice. However, it is seldom clear from published articles in *Groupwork* whether and/or how contributors have searched the literature and this could become one standard for future practice and its dissemination.

Adapting work on levels of outcomes of educational programmes (Kirkpatrick, 1967; Barr et al, 2000; Carpenter, 2004), it is possible to see how evaluation may focus on:

- Groupworkers' and/or members' reactions: Their views of, and satisfaction with a group, as it evolves over time and looking back on the experience
- Modification in attitudes: Changes in how they perceive their needs, problems and ways forward, and what facilitated such movement
- Acquisition of knowledge and skills: Changes in how they approach problem solving and decision-making, and what facilitated such shifts
- Behavioural change: What groupworkers and/or members actually do differently, and what facilitates and blocks such difference
- Organisational change: The impact of the group on other stakeholders
- Benefits to group members, their carers and those they care for: Improvements in well-being that may be attributed to the group.

It is seldom clear from published articles in *Groupwork* what persuaded contributors to explore which of the processes and outcomes just outlined. Such analysis could become a second standard for future practice and its dissemination.

Manor (2003) describes a process where group members were enabled to identify their goals and then engaged in analysing which learning experiences might promote their realisation. From here it is a small step to delineating the indicators that might suggest movement towards goal achievement (see Preston-Shoot, 1988, for a similar approach). Stating group and individual objectives in terms of processes by which it is hoped the group will be characterised, and outcomes that are expected, is key to aligning evaluation with goals. Connecting evaluation methods with sought goals could become a third standard for future practice and its dissemination.

A fourth standard might be triangulation, expanding how evaluation can inform theory and practice by combining methods in order partly to overcome their individual shortcomings. Towl and Dexter (1994) make this point when discussing their use of psychometric evaluation of anger management courses. Connecting use of standardised instruments with biographical information, qualitative data, and follow-up interviews would enable a much richer understanding of what is actually working, for whom, to what degree and for how long.

A fifth standard relates to the number of times the frequencies are opened. Despite guidance that identifies evaluation as an aspect of preparation for, and beginning to work with groups (Preston-Shoot, 1988), groupworkers appear still to approach it as an ending task, part of the termination phase (Hadlow, 1995; Ross, 1991; Szmagalski, 1989/90). Indeed, such an approach is codified in one set of standards (AASWG, 1999). Such an approach, which is sometimes related to a lack of resources for integrating assessment and evaluation from the outset (Craig, 1988), is likely to restrict what can be meaningfully said about group process and outcomes because baseline measures and repeated quantitative and/or qualitative monitoring will not have been used. For example, Grindley (1994) used questionnaires to note changes in behaviour and emotions but only as an end rating and self-report. This limits what may be derived as benefits from the group. Lebacq and Shah (1989) record and evaluate sessions, including reviews with parents and children, but no baseline measures were taken, again limiting what change may be attributed to the group experience. Mistry's groupwork account (1989) is similar, making it difficult to establish the degree of change in group members' confidence and skills. In none of these examples was follow-up data obtained so it is impossible to know whether progress was maintained after the groups closed.

The transporter room

The literature does contain examples of where evidence can transport groupwork theory and practice. In relation to what may be termed inputs, the opportunities provided by working in groups, Mullender (1995) and Berger (1997-98) provide examples of post group interviews and questionnaires that focus on what members liked and gained, what they had expected and what worked best, coupled with what recommendations for improvement they would make. With this approach Szmagalski (1989/90) triangulates indicators of observed behaviour.

Monitoring group process over time can be achieved through reviewing monthly objectives (Muir and Notta, 1993) and through observed behaviour, both inside the group but also between members outside it. Monitoring group content over time can be achieved through the use of open-ended evaluation questions at the end of each session (Read et al, 2000), which enables emerging themes to be expressed by group members and/or facilitators.

Individual outcomes can be tracked by measurement scales (for examples, see Otway and Peake, 1994; Mullender, 1995), preferably taken at several points before, during and after the group. Personal statements and groupworker reports may also be used (Ni Chorcora et al, 1994; Dixon and Phillips, 1994). Group and organizational change outcomes can be traced using short term and long term appraisals by members, enabling benefits to be identified against initial objectives (see Taylor et al, 1988, for an example drawn from a team development exercise). Finally, the impact of group experience can be assessed by means of follow-up, with group members and/or referrers reporting back (see Hadlow, 1995).

To boldly go where few groupworkers have gone before

The theme of this article is metanoia – a shift of mind. It is urging the crew of Star Ship Groupwork to reconfigure evaluation as an omnipresent focus throughout groupwork practice, and to transport it from a preoccupation with a single point description to a systematic application of a range of tools at various time points, selected to be consistent with the type of group.

This shift of mind will require self-examination, as groupworkers reflect on their attitudes towards travelling in this space, review groupwork's conceptual base against emerging evidence, and consider the standards for effective knowledge-informed practice by which they should be held accountable. It will also require participative openness with other travellers, debating what counts as evidence, as change, as approved practice, and as success. It will also require engaging in policy and practice leadership with Star Fleet Command, disseminating findings and seeking to transform both practice space and its frontiers. In so doing new questions will be generated, new curiosities to be explored.

Energise

This article does not pretend that, for groupwork to live long and prosper, systematic evaluation is the sole crystal. It does venture to suggest that it is *one* crystal and that, in defining the groupwork galaxy as a space for evaluation, groupwork skills and knowledge can be accessed as research tools. Moreover, it is founded on the belief that systematic reviews of the literature and of practice will help to energise Star Ship Groupwork's theoretical base and position as a transformative force.

References

AASWG (1999) *Standards for Social Work Practice with Groups*. Akron, OH: Association for the Advancement of Social Work with Groups

Barnes, B., Ernst, S. and Hyde, K. (1999) *An Introduction to Groupwork. A Group-analytic perspective*. Basingstoke: Palgrave

Barnes, J. (2002) *Focus on the Future: Key Messages from Focus Groups about the Future of Social Work training*. London: Department of Health

Barnett, S., Corder, F. and Jehu, D. (1990) Group treatment for women sex offenders against children. *Groupwork*, 3, 2, 191-203

Barr, H., Freeth, D., Hammick, M., Koppel, I. and Reeves, S. (2000) *Evaluating Interprofessional Education: A United Kingdom review for health and social care*. London: BERA/CAIPE

Berger, R. (1997-98) Suddenly the light went on: Using groupwork to empower returning students. *Groupwork*, 10, 1, 21-29

Brown, A. (1996) Groupwork into the future: Some personal reflections. *Groupwork*, 9, 1, 80-96

Caddick, B. (1991 Using groups in working with offenders: A survey of groupwork in the probation services of England and Wales. *Groupwork*, 4, 3, 197-214

Carpenter, J. (2004) How can we evaluate the outcomes of social work education. Paper given at the Social Work Education Conference, Glasgow, 8th July

Clarke, P. and Aimable, A. (1990) Groupwork techniques in a residential primary school for emotionally disturbed boys. *Groupwork*, 3, 1, 36-48

Cowburn, M. (1990) Work with male sex offenders in groups. *Groupwork*, 3, 2, 157-171

Craig, E. (1990) Starting the journey: enhancing the therapeutic elements of groupwork for adolescent female child sexual abuse victims. *Groupwork*, 3, 2, 103-117

Craig, R. (1988) Structured activities with adolescent boys. *Groupwork*, 1, 1, 48-59

Cwikel, J. and Oron, A. (1991 A long-term support group for chronic schizophrenic outpatients: a quantitative and qualitative evaluation. *Groupwork*, 4, 2, 163-177

DeLois, K. (2003) Genderbending: Reflections on group work with queer youth. in M. Cohen and A. Mullender (Eds.) *Gender and Groupwork*. London: Routledge

Department of Health (1998) *Modernising Social Services*. London: TSO

Dixon, G. and Phillips, M. (1994) A psychotherapeutic group for boys who have been sexually abused. *Groupwork*, 7, 1, 79-95

Doel, M. and Sawdon, C. (1999) *The Essential Groupworker. Teaching and learning creative groupwork*. London: Jessica Kingsley

Douglas, T. (1991) *A Handbook of Common Groupwork Problems*. London: Routledge

Douglas, T. (2000) *Basic Groupwork* (2nd ed). London: Routledge

Gallant, W., Gallant, M., Gorey, K., Holosko, M. and Siegel, S. (1997-98) The use of music in group work with out-patient alcoholic couples: A pilot investigation. *Groupwork*, 10, 2, 155-174

Garrett, P. (1995) Group dialogue within prisons. *Groupwork*, 8, 1, 49-66

Gillam, T. (2003) An isle full of noises: Enhancing mental health through the Music Workshop Project. *Groupwork*, 13, 3, 45-64

Gordon, K. (1992) Evaluation for the improvement of groupwork practice. *Groupwork*, 5, 1, 34-49

Grindley, G. (1994) Working with religious communities. *Groupwork*, 7, 1, 50-62

Habermann, U. (1993 Why groupwork is not put into practice: Reflections on the social work scene in Denmark. *Groupwork*, 6, 1, 17-29

Hadlow, J. (1995 Groupwork to facilitate family reconstitution: A social work response. *Groupwork*, 8, 3, 313-323

Harry, R., Hegarty, P., Lisles, C., Thurston, R. and Vanstone, M. (1997-98) Research into practice does go: Integrating research within programme development. *Groupwork*, 10, 2, 107-125

Heap, K. (1992) The European groupwork scene: Where were we? Where are we? Where are we going? *Groupwork*, 5, 1, 9-23

Hill, A. (2001) 'No-one else could understand': Women's experiences of a support group run by and for mothers of sexually abused children. *British Journal of Social Work*, 31, 3, 385-397

Hopmeyer, E. and Werk, A. (1993) A comparative study of four family bereavement groups. *Groupwork*, 6, 2, 107-121

Humphreys, C., Berridge, D., Butler, I. and Ruddick, R. (2003) Making research count: The development of knowledge-based practice. *Research Policy and Planning*, 21, 1, 11-19

IASSW (2001) International Definition of Social Work. Copenhagen: International Association of Schools of Social Work and the International Federation of Social Workers

Johnson, P., Beckerman, A, and Auerbach, C. (2001) Researching our own practice: Single system design for groupwork. *Groupwork*, 13, 1, 57-72

Kirkpatrick, D. (1967) Evaluation of training. in R. Craig and L. Bittel (Eds.) *Training and Development Handbook*. New York: McGraw-Hill

Kolbo, J., Horn, K. and Randall, E. (1997-98) Implementing a novel groupwork model: Application of an innovation-developmental process. *Groupwork*, 10, 1, 41-54

Kurland, R. and Salmon, R. (1993) Groupwork versus casework in a group. *Groupwork*, 6, 1, 5-16

Lebacq, M. and Shah, Z. (1989) A group for black and white sexually abused children. *Groupwork*, 2, 2, 123-133

Lee, F. (2000) Working with natural groups of youth-at-risk: An RGC approach. *Groupwork*, 12, 3, 21-36

Maggs-Rapport, F. (2000) Teenagers' experiences of a health promotion project. *Groupwork*, 12, 3, 5-20

Manor, O. (2003) Groupwork fit for purpose? An inclusive framework for mental health. *Groupwork*, 13, 3, 101-128

Marsh, P. and Triseliotis, J. (1996) *Ready to Practise? Social workers and probation officers: Their training and first year in work*. Aldershot: Avebury

Masson, H. and Erooga, M. (1990) The forgotten parent: Groupwork with mothers of sexually abused children. *Groupwork*, 3, 2, 144-156

Mathias-Williams, R. and Thomas, N. (2002) Great expectations? The career aspirations of social work students. *Social Work Education*, 21, 4, 421-435

Matzat, J. (1993) Away with experts? Self-help groupwork in Germany. *Groupwork*, 6, 1, 30-42

McKernan McKay, M., Garcia, T., Scally, J. and Martinez, L. (1996) A collaborative group approach for urban parents. *Groupwork*, 9, 1, 15-26

Mistry, T. (1989) Establishing a feminist model of groupwork in the probation service. *Groupwork*, 2, 2, 145-158

Muir, L. and Notta, H. (1993) An Asian mother's group. *Groupwork*, 6, 2, 122-132

Mullender, A. (1988) Groupwork as the method of choice with black children in white foster homes. *Groupwork*, 1, 2, 158-172

Mullender, A. (1995) Groups for children who have lived with domestic violence: Learning from North America. *Groupwork*, 8, 1, 79-98

Mullender, A. (1996) Groupwork with male 'domestic' abusers: Models and dilemmas. *Groupwork*, 9, 1, 27-47

Mullender, A. and Ward, D. (1991) *Self-Directed Groupwork: Users take action for empowerment*. London: Whiting and Birch

Mulvie, C. (1991) Groupwork in the Luton probation and bail hostel. *Groupwork*, 4, 3, 249-261

Ni Chorcora, M., Jennings, E. and Lordan, N. (1994) Issues of empowerment: anti-oppressive groupwork by disabled people in Ireland. *Groupwork*, 7, 1, 63-78

O'Connor, I. (1992) Bereaved by suicide: Setting up an 'ideal' therapy group in a real world. *Groupwork*, 5, 3, 74-86

Otway, O. and Peake, A. (1994) Using a facilitated self help group for women whose children have been sexually abused. *Groupwork*, 7, 2, 153-162

Papps, B., Manor, O. and Carson, J. (2003) Using groupwork in community mental health: Practitioners' views. *Groupwork*, 13, 3, 6-36

Pawson, R., Boaz, A., Grayson, L., Long, A. and Barnes, C. (2003) *Types and Quality of Knowledge in Social Care*. London: Social Care Institute for Excellence

Peake, A. and Otway, O. (1990) Evaluating success in groupwork: Why not measure the obvious?' *Groupwork*, 3, 2, 118-133

Pennells, M. (1995) Time and space to grieve: A bereavement group for children. *Groupwork*, 8, 3, 243-254

Phillips, J. (2001) *Groupwork in Social Care*. London: Jessica Kingsley Publishers

Pollio, D. (2002) The evidence-based group worker. *Social Work with Groups*, 25, 4, 57-70

Preston-Shoot, M. (1988) A model for evaluating groupwork. *Groupwork*, 1, 2, 147-157

Preston-Shoot, M. (2004) Responding by degrees: surveying the education and practice landscape. *Social Work Education*, 23, 6, 667-692

QAA (2000) *Subject Benchmark Statements: Social Policy and Administration and Social Work*. Gloucester: The Quality Assurance Agency for Higher Education

Read, S., Papakosta-Harvey, V. and Bower, S. (2000) Using workshops on loss for adults with learning disabilities. *Groupwork*, 12, 2, 6-26

Reid, K. (1988) 'But I don't want to lead a group!' Some common problems of social workers leading groups. *Groupwork*, 1, 2, 124-134

Rhule, C. (1988) A group for white women with black children. *Groupwork*, 1, 1, 41-47

Ross, S. (1991) The termination phase in groupwork: tasks for the groupworker. *Groupwork*, 4, 10, 57-70

Schneewind, E. (1996) Support groups for families of confused elders: issues surrounding open peer-led groups. *Groupwork*, 9, 3, 303-319

Senior, P. (1991) Groupwork in the probation service: care or control in the 1990s. *Groupwork*, 4, 3, 284-295

Shulman, L. (1988) Groupwork practice with hard to reach clients: a modality of choice. *Groupwork*, 1, 1, 5-16

Szmagalski, J. (1989-90) Staff development through groupwork in Polish community agencies: The 'Centres of Culture'. *Groupwork*, 2, 3, 237-247

Taylor, J., Miles, D. and Eastgate, J. (1988) A team development exercise. *Groupwork*, 1, 3, 252-261

TOPSS (2002) *The National Occupational Standards for Social Work*. Leeds: Training Organisation for the Personal Social Services

Towl, G. and Dexter, P. (1994) Anger management groupwork with prisoners: An empirical evaluation. *Groupwork*, 7, 3, 256-269

Tribe, R. and Fitzgerald, J. (1989) A way forward: A group for refugee women. *Groupwork*, 2, 2, 159-166

Ward, A. (1995) Establishing community meetings in a children's home. *Groupwork*, 8, 1, 67-78

Ward, D. (2002) Groupwork. in R. Adams, L. Dominelli and M. Payne (Eds.) *Social Work: Themes, issues and critical debates*. Basingstoke: Palgrave

Weisen, R. (1991) Evaluative study of groupwork for stress and anxiety.

Groupwork, 4, 2, 152-162

Whitaker, D. (2001) *Using Groups to Help People*. (2nd ed) London: Routledge

Whitaker, D. and Archer, L. (1994) Partnership research and its contributions to learning and to team-building. *Social Work Education*, 13, 3, 39-60

Wintram, C., Chamberlain, K., Kuhn, M. and Smith, J. (1994) A time for women: An account of a group for women on an out of city housing development in Leicester. *Groupwork*, 7, 2, 125-135

Worden, B. (2000) Using fieldwork experience as a tool for teaching: a multi-layered approach. *Groupwork*, 12, 3, 56-76

Appendix: Finding crystals

Craig (1998) describes how group members and workers evaluated each session and its different components, extrapolating perspectives on effectiveness.

Mullender (1988) uses discussion, experiential exercises, games and listening to establish a baseline. She then tracks changes in how young people referred to themselves and in their levels of cultural knowledge. What is less clear, because of the absence of follow-up, is whether identified changes endured.

Craig (1990) describes the use of contracts, with group members and referring social workers, as the means to establish a baseline of issues to be worked on. Both referring social workers and group members assess movement through rating exercises and proformas in order to establish the effects of the programme. The need for follow-up to evaluate the longer-term benefits of the group is acknowledged.

Masson and Erooga (1990) use a self-administered questionnaire, which focuses on group members' self concept, in an early and then concluding group session. This approach appears to have enabled the group to identify where there had (not) been individual change and to hypothesise about reasons for this. This evidence was triangulated with feedback from members about the group experience.

Barnett and colleagues (1990) measure outcomes by therapist records of sessions and client evaluation sheets. Before and after attending the group, members completed a cognitions scale. The article reviews the degree of reliance that may be placed on self-report, arguing that triangulation of data enables identification of consistency of results. The need for long-term follow up is noted.

Weisen (1991) uses an anxiety inventory and a coping questionnaire, administered pre and post group, to provide evidence for effectiveness and therapeutic value. A control group was an added feature of this study but this was only roughly matched to the study group.

Cwikel and Oron (1991) evaluate a group for people with severe mental health problems retrospectively in terms of number of readmissions into hospital and drug dosage before and during the group. When compared with comparable individuals who were not group members, some benefit is attributed to group membership.

Hopmeyer and Werk (1993) undertake a comparative study of bereavement groups in order to improve services and to develop a training manual. Members of four groups were asked to complete an adapted version of a social support network questionnaire. The results illustrate how groups enable people to accomplish grief work and to create support networks.

Towl and Dexter (1994) utilise psychometric evaluation in anger management courses and discuss the strengths and weaknesses of several other methods – other report, behavioural checklists and questionnaires. The results of one anger management group are presented using the inventory. Selection for groups is linked to the choice of appropriate types of evaluation.

McKernan McKay and colleagues (1996) offer a theoretically and empirically based groupwork approach for work with parents. Measures of parenting stress, parenting practice, and relationships with children were taken in the first group session. These measures are then used alongside group interaction to enable group members to make changes. As the paper presents in part a theoretical model, data from the end of the group is not offered.

Harry and colleagues (1997-98) present an integrated and continuous process of groupwork practice and evaluation with offenders. A range of data collection methods is used, some pre and post group, including satisfaction questionnaires, interviews with all stakeholders, offender profiles, attendance records, reconviction rates and attitude change scales.

Gallant and colleagues (1997-98) administer a questionnaire that included a psychosocial screening inventory before and after group sessions. Their paper presents the results in terms of groupwork effects and content analysis of sessions, to demonstrate the benefits from the intervention

.

Lee (2000), working with natural groups of young people at risk, uses questionnaires and individual interviews to generate guidelines for promoting more effective intervention with this population.

Worden (2000) tests students before and after a course teaching groupwork method. This shows a significant increase of self-confidence in learning.

Data is presented to show differences in student response pre and post course relating to knowledge of environmental obstacles, group roles, group development and the need for preparation.

Johnson and colleagues (2001) describe and discuss, with examples, a single system design for monitoring practice.

Gillam (2003) researches the effectiveness of a music workshop project for people with a range of mental health problems. The aims of the research are identified and questionnaires are used for project members, other service users and staff. The paper offers a critique of different research methods and discusses implications for the project derived from the data.

Papps and colleagues (2003) report the views of mental health professionals on the use of groupwork, derived from a questionnaire. Results are reported about the outcomes of groupwork, methods, and factors that help and hinder practice. They offer a critique of surveys of this type.

As stated the article set out to review materials published in *Groupwork*. However, one article published in *Social Work with Groups* (Pollio, 2002) provides an interesting parallel. Pollio argues that groupworkers must systematically appraise all available evidence, so he spreads the net widely to include effectiveness studies, quasi-experimental designs, narratives, focus groups and case studies. He further argues that practitioners should have time to learn and thereby build their knowledge.

This chapter first published in 2004 in *Groupwork* Vol. 14(3), pp.18-43

At the time of writing, the author was Head of Department of Applied Social Studies, University of Luton

A version of this article was presented under the same title at the 10th European Groupwork Symposium, York, England, July 2004, 'What Counts as Evidence in Groupwork?'

Researching groupwork: Outsider and insider perspectives

Fiona McDermott

Abstract: *The focus of this paper is on providing a frame for developing research designs for groupwork practice. Two designs are described – one referring to the researcher who adopts an 'outside' location, and the other for an 'insider' or researcher-group-work-practitioner. Issues of epistemology, methodology, ethics and methods are raised, as are considerations of existing gaps in research knowledge. Practitioners and researchers are encouraged to think more creatively about the kinds of methods which could be used when approaching such a dynamic, complex and fascinating subject as the workings and benefits of group participation.*

Keywords: *practitioner research; outcome; research design; groupwork*

Introduction

There are now more calls to firmly establish groupwork as a location for research (Preston-Shoot, 2004b), and, given that the research base for groupwork is advancing with a developing interest in evidence based interventions (Pollio, 2002), it has become increasingly imperative that we (as groupworkers) contribute. This is easier said than done: many groupworkers do not see themselves as researchers and fear they lack the skills to do justice to systematically communicating their knowledge about the work which their group has achieved.

In this paper, I will sketch the nature of some of the issues (epistemological, methodological) facing those who wish to research group programs, and then propose a research frame which can be brought to bear in developing a research design. Two 'ideal typical' research designs are described, one relating to 'outsider' or researcher-only research, and the other to 'insider' or researcher-practitioner research.

The paper concludes with some suggestions about the need to be more creative in research designs, and for research addressing the more obvious gaps in our knowledge of who may benefit from groupwork programs.

Researching groups: Issues facing researchers

The most striking characteristic of all groups is their complexity – the multiple 'layers' of intersecting interaction and fluid meanings which occur over time, and within a context, and which all go into making the experience and the process of a group. Everyone in a group becomes both participant and observer, power shifts as meanings are constructed, negotiated, challenged or allowed to prevail.

Not surprisingly, how to understand and/or measure what is going on in a group challenges any research design (see for example, discussions of methodological problems in researching groupwork in Nietzel et al, 1987; Bloch, 1988; Krause and Howard, 1999; Edmonds et al, 1999; Westbury and Tutty, 1999; Borkovec and Miranda, 1999; McKenzie, 2001; Kanas, 2001). Issues of particular significance include questions about research designs – whether process or outcome is to be studied, whether comparisons between individual and group interventions are more revealing of benefits and limitations, how participants can be followed up, the multiple variables which may influence outcome (group leader and group participant characteristics, the severity of problems which bring people to a group, the motivation of participants, the social support available to them, etc.).

A primary but difficult decision – namely, what is to count as evidence – does however, take us into heavily contested terrain. The validity and reliability, the trustworthiness and authenticity of evidence is determined by the researcher's epistemological position, what we might think of as the researcher's beliefs about the nature of social reality. In fact the use of these terms – reliability and validity, authenticity and trustworthiness – tells us a great deal about the researcher's epistemological positioning.

Generally, different epistemological positions are identified as positivist, interpretivist, and critical. Although there is not scope here to go into detailed discussion about epistemology and paradigms for research, suffice to say that positivist research draws on natural science models to study elements in the social world with the purpose of discovering rules underpinning social phenomena; interpretivist epistemology originates in social constructivist perspectives which emphasise that meaning-making is central to our perceptions of social reality and our actions in the social world; critical theoretical perspectives take a view of social reality as structured by a history of struggle over the distribution of power and resources. As an example of these epistemological differences, if the title of this paper had been 'How do we measure outcomes of group interventions' this suggests a positivist frame. Within an interpretivist frame the title might be something like 'The meaning of groupwork for leaders and participants: exploring outcomes'. Within a critical theory frame it might read – 'What works for whom in groupwork?'

In terms of what would constitute evidence within each paradigm, in the first – positivist – reliability and validity of evidence relies solely on the soundness and quality of the methodology and methods used. In the second – interpretivist – emphasis is on the transparency of the process of doing the research to reveal trustworthy and authentic data interpretations capturing the meaning of the experience for participants. In the third – critical – the methods and process of the research are important to the extent that what is admitted as evidence is theoretically-driven.

In this paper my focus will be on positivist and interpretivist positions. For the former, the experimental design is the exemplar of positivist research. In the latter, there is greater variety in designs but they are chiefly those that rely on description, observation and interaction with the researched.

Positivist research designs

What can be observed in much group focused research is that it is very often designed for groups which *are* researchable, that is, where the group intervention can be controlled for a particular population. This tends to exclude a number of other kinds of groups, or in the case of long term, often psychoanalytically-oriented groups, makes them especially problematic from a research design perspective.

By controlling the group effect to be studied, researchers attempt to compare like with like in relation to a time-limited intervention. For this reason, the majority of empirical studies focus on short-term interventions with homogenous populations. Hence there is a preponderance of studies looking at the impact of group models that are derived from Cognitive Behavioural theory. This means that there are a substantial number of studies of groups which are structured and may use psychoeducational, skill-based and/or manualised interventions in short term groups. However, the findings from studies of short-term group interventions do provide evidence for their efficacy (favourable outcomes in clinical trials), applicability and efficiency (Piper and Joyce, 1996).

The literature contains a number of examples of Randomised Controlled Trials – usually cited as the 'gold standard' of evidence on outcome within positivist epistemology. However, the Randomised

Controlled Trial may be neither possible in its most rigorous form, nor particularly desirable in relation to research on groups. RCTs are designed to exclude rather than include such contextual factors as the organisational setting of the group, the role of family, work and friendships in sustaining (or otherwise) individuals, factors which may be of considerable significance in assessing the gains or losses associated with participation in a group (see Donenberg, 1999; also Wilberg and Karterud, 2001). Long term, open groups pose further difficulties for RCT designs in economic and practical terms as Steiner et al (2001, p.422) point out. Harding and Higginson (2003) comment critically in relation to the use of RCTs in cancer and palliative care research because patients in such groups are sick and vulnerable and the ethics of subjecting them to RCTs is highly questionable. Further, it is also the case that the RCT methodology is suitable for measuring particular kinds of therapeutic interventions such as CBT thus leading to an evidence base biased in the direction of more structured, closed and short term programs (see McDermott, 2003).

Within the practice literature on groupwork, ideas have been put forward to encourage and assist groupworkers to think about the extent to which their groups are achieving espoused objectives. Yalom (1975) and later Bloch and Aveline (1996, pp.93-98) have, for example, proposed that there are a number of 'curative factors' at work in all groups, regardless of treatment modality, for example, group cohesiveness, learning from interpersonal action, insight, universality, generation of hope, etc.

These factors refer particularly to issues of group process and as such, refer principally to the less tangible but often especially fulfilling aspects of group participation. However, how to operationalise them for purposes of measuring outcome is quite problematic, given their conceptual ambiguity and the attendant difficulty of establishing whether there is a cause-effect relationship between these elements and outcomes for individuals.

Interpretivist research designs

In the literature there is less evidence of published studies using interpretivist designs. Research which relies on observational, descriptive and interactional methods – as we know – continues to struggle for acceptance and recognition within scientific journals. (However there are some exceptions to this: see for example the October, 1996 edition of *Australasian Psychiatry*, and papers in discipline-specific journals such as this journal as well as *Social Work Practice with Groups*). Interpretivist research can at times lack rigour and take the form of reportage rather than analysis: the fault here lies with researchers rather than epistemology or methodology. However, its acceptance is often hampered by criteria for research adequacy being applied to it which originate with positivist research rather than criteria relevant to the interpretivist paradigm. (For a full discussion of criteria for evaluating interpretivist research see Fossey et al, 2002.)

Interestingly, the qualitative methods most often used in interpretivist designs – interviewing, observing, attention to process, interpreting meaning – suggest that groupworkers (and social workers in particular) are especially suited to undertaking this kind of research. We should build on our strengths!

A highly noteworthy absence in the literature is reference to or studies of how group participants measure outcome or effectiveness. Where these are noted, they are in the form of anecdotes or comments from satisfaction surveys, often used to promote what might be called 'smiling evaluations' (Preston-Shoot, 2004a) which encourage 'good feelings' in group participants and researchers, and maybe funding bodies. Group participants' views are rarely taken seriously or judged to comprise evidence of outcome.

Finding a research frame

Given all the foregoing, how are we to go about researching outcome in groupwork practice? Perhaps we can most usefully begin by finding a frame and a focus for our research plan. Regardless of the kind of research we want to do, we need to pose and answer the following questions:

- *Why measure or research outcome?*
- *Who should do it?*
- *When – what time frame?*
- *Where – what is the context?*
- *Ethical considerations?*
- *What is to be measured or researched?*
- *What is to constitute evidence?*

Why, in the first place, do we want to measure or research outcomes in groupwork?

We can identify a number of compelling reasons:

- To establish evidence – to know 'what works', 'what works for whom', 'what doesn't work'
- To establish accountability – to funders, service users, service providers
- To close the gaps in what is known, or to open up areas where we do not know
- To improve our practice and the effectiveness of what we do – to benefit those for whom groupwork is the chosen intervention
- To change practice if that is indicated. This might mean being prepared to do things differently if the evidence from research is contrary to our beliefs: to avoid stopping with the 'smiling evaluation'

Who should do the research or the evaluation? Whose group is it?

There are many stakeholders to any group evaluation – group participants, group leaders, funding bodies, the community more generally. And there are advantages and disadvantages arising from the different positioning of different stakeholders to the evaluation, for example funding bodies want value-for-money which often suggests that they are looking for short-term, more immediate benefits; leaders want to see that their work is effective; participants may want to be cured, or to be helped, or to 'do their time'; communities want to see that the group program deals with disruptive or problematic behaviours, or at the least, reduces the risk of them occurring. Communities might also want to see their usefulness in building cohesion and bonds between people. Researcher/practitioners may want to focus on research-generated knowledge to enable them to 'go on' as group leaders. These are very different agendas and suggest very different goals, aims, objectives and methods of evaluating a group. And they also indicate potentially very different standards for what will constitute evidence that these objectives are being met.

When should it be done, when should outcomes be measured?

Evaluation should be an intrinsic and ongoing aspect of groupwork, there from the beginning, built into the program or milieu. More often than not – and sometimes reflecting the source from which the wish to measure originated – evaluation is an ending activity, tacked on, usually in the guise of a 'satisfaction survey' or exit interview. While this is useful in providing a snapshot of what is or has happened, it is limited in its ability to generate more substantial knowledge. Other methods, for example, ongoing surveys or interviews with participants and the use of standardized measures at various time points (pre-group, beginning, middle, end, and at post-group), can provide greater quantity and quality of data for analysis.

How can it be done ethically?

Ethical considerations, like the evaluation itself, must be part of the process from the beginning. Usually, group programs are offered to people who are in some sense vulnerable e.g. unwell, disabled, managing their lives with difficulty, engaging in problematic behaviour (criminality, substance abuse). They may be either voluntary or involuntary group participants. Particular ethical considerations refer to the freedom of subjects to participate or not in the research, to not be harmed (physically, emotionally) by the research, and to be able to consent to the research only after all aspects of it have been fully explained to them. (For a thought-provoking discussion of ethical issues in groupwork research, see Lewis, 2004).

The tension here is balancing tendencies (and interference) from the forces of the 'nanny state' with genuine need to protect and minimise harm (Harding and Higginson, 2003). This means that researchers should consider using methods that are, by and large, non-intrusive and not requiring participants to do more than they are comfortable with or more than is required to answer the research questions.

Where should it be done?

The context in which a group outcome is measured is highly significant. It does make a difference whether the group is part of a model or demonstration program, a RCT or replication study, is part of an in-patient or out-patient program, occurs in private practice or as a community-based program. Different contexts make different kinds of evaluations possible, limiting some aspects, facilitating others. So, it is important to think about how the influence of context might be accounted for in the research, for example, whether the group under study is one amongst a number of programs participants engage in, whether participants have support for their participation from families, etc.

What is it that is being measured or evaluated?

How this question will be answered takes us back through all the earlier questions. It is a question about epistemologies, about values, about what outcome the group has been established to achieve and in whose interests the group exists in the first place. Whether it will be measured as achieving its objective will depend on what the group's objective was in the first place. This is not as straightforward as it sounds as there are always objectives which are *not* specified, or objectives which evolve, or unexpected objectives, or unintended outcomes. Is the objective of the group to cure patients, to control them and their behaviour, to support and maintain them in their everyday lives, to change them? A group might have all of these as its objectives, or several of them. It may even have contradictory objectives, or mutually exclusive objectives, and there may not be consensus amongst the many stakeholders on what precisely these objectives are. But it is vital that efforts are made to, at the least, recognise and identify what are the likely objectives which are to be measured/evaluated.

The question about what is to be measured is further complicated by whether our focus is on changes that participants make as a result of the group, or whether our focus is on understanding and measuring the group processes that are causal in effecting changes, e.g. the role of the leaders, the theoretical base, the interactions of participants, the structure of the group, etc. Distinguishing these foci at the outset is crucial.

What is to constitute evidence?

As we noted earlier, the question of what constitutes evidence is essentially an epistemological one. Different research designs emanate from different epistemological positions and the acceptance of data as evidence is determined by those understandings of ontology and methodology with their attendant rules and guidelines for methods of data collection, data analysis and interpretation. For example, comments from participants might be accepted as evidence within interpretivist research, drawing as it does on social constructivist perspectives, but are unlikely to be part of an experimental design – except when 'translated' into some other objective and measurable form.

From the frame to the design

These questions then, are proposed as a kind of orientation frame which helps us to clarify our research focus and our research stance prior to the development of a research question and design. I shall now consider how we might go about measuring outcome in a group.

There are two different researcher 'locations' which we could adopt, the researcher as 'researcher-only' or 'outsider' and the 'practitioner-researcher' or 'insider'. These locations are separate and very different but can serve a similar and shared purpose, principally that of building groupwork as a recognised and vibrant site of research, informed by and augmented by the 'view' from both locations – inside and outside. Personally and professionally, I am interested in what we can learn and combine from both, but I am myself, as a practising groupworker, more a 'practitioner-researcher' or 'insider' than a 'researcher-only' or 'outsider'.

I want to sketch here the kinds of 'ideal typical' research that might emerge from each research location. However, it is important to emphasise that, regardless of the insider or outsider location of the researcher, the measuring and evaluation task must begin with a clear conceptual focus, one which has arrived at answers to the questions posed earlier.

'Researcher-only', 'outsider' research

Measuring group outcome can be best served by the adoption of quasi-experimental, flexible research designs which include observational elements. So here the argument is for groupwork researchers to take the middle ground between positivist and interpretivist research designs, (sometimes called post positivist) utilising both quantitative and qualitative methods.

This would proceed from a multi-dimensional perspective, recognising that there are many stakeholders to every group – leaders, participants, funding bodies, communities. Each has a valid and valuable perspective. In fact, the researcher's first task is to align the evaluation with the goals the group has been established to meet. As we saw earlier this means being alert to the multiple goals, objectives and consequences likely to attend the group's evolution, as well as an understanding of the theoretical position underpinning the group's design. It suggests a parallel focus on process and outcome which requires the use of multiple methods of data gathering – a systematic literature review, standardized scales, observation, self-reports from leaders, participants, significant others (which might include other people in the organisation, other service providers, family members, etc.), interviews and questionnaires.

Very importantly, we would want to establish some kind of baseline at the beginning of the group in a way which can allow for the tracking of changes within the group over time which can be attributed to the group itself, for example, standardised scales measuring depression or quality of life at several time points, e.g before, during and after group participation. Follow-up interviews and assessment for participants is a key element, indicating the extent to which the group intervention led to sustained changes.

The interpretation of data would arise from combining findings arrived at through all these methods – a bit like opening different windows onto group phenomena. Data interpretation would not seek to undercut findings from different 'windows' but rather to use them in combination as reflecting (or illuminating) different facets of the whole. This might mean that differences and contradictions appear in the data. Interpretation would then rely on making sense of these as reflecting different aspects of group elements which, in combination, refer to and allow the complexity and multifaceted nature of the enterprise to emerge.

'Researcher practitioner', 'insider' research

Group workers are often not researchers but rather practitioners who rely on the accretion of practice wisdom in deciding what works for whom. Kanas (2001, p.290) comments: '... the best evidence for the clinician is his or her own results with prior patients similar to the one being considered, or the results of similar therapists in similar settings with similar patients receiving similar treatment'. However, every group can also be thought of as an ongoing process of research-in-action: indeed groups owe their vitality and energy to the fact that they are continually researching themselves. As Long (1992, p.78) points out, groups '... constantly interact with the results of their own observations'. In fact, they can be thought of as exemplifying participatory action research (McTaggart, 1993; Wadsworth, 1997), characterised by a cycle of action, reflection on that action, further action. This is the case regardless of the type of group or the time frame it has adopted. A psychotherapy group may assist a participant to think through an important decision but in the process others will be engaged in re-viewing their own ways of thinking and acting, weighing up whether or not the group is able to help them.

Considering groups to be sites of research-in-action also alerts us to what Long (1992, p.79) refers to as a 'data problem'. Because the meanings of actions and processes within the group are not self-evident but rather emerge through the exchanges and interactions taking place amongst participants, we need to understand the context (both internal and external to the group) and how it is being constructed and interpreted in the minds of participants.

As practitioners evaluating our groups, we can identify ourselves as 'insider' researchers with a location that both obscures elements of what is happening as well as enriches our perspective. From this location we might give central importance to the concept of 'Thinking Group', that is, working from the perspective of the group-as-a-whole, focusing on the *group* as the unit of attention and analysis rather than on individuals. While we may identify changes that individuals achieve, what these mean and how they were arrived at refer specifically to the nature and interpretation made of the experience of working together. Individuals working together can be studied as such, from the viewpoint that there is some kind of relationship between individuals in a group which may account for the changes we observe or assert have occurred for individuals (McDermott, 2002, pp.195-206).

In studying the group's progress there are a number of observable signs indicative of the extent and way in which the group is working. These refer to the extent to which the group is achieving its purposes – for individuals and for the collective; what is happening over time, for example, how are individuals and the group as a whole changing over time. Importantly, how we pose, interpret and make sense of these observable signs will depend on the theoretical and knowledge base that informs our practice.

As described earlier, the group can be thought of as synonymous with the cycles ascribed to participatory action research – action, reflection on action, further action. Sharpening one's observational and listening skills with this framework in mind, provides access to feedback about where the process is heading and how and to what extent it is achieving the group's purpose. The skills which practitioners already possess are also skills which can be brought to the research endeavour – understanding process, making interpretations/analysing data.

Deriving credible evidence by analyzing and interpreting data for the insider, practitioner-researcher, is only problematic if we apply criteria derived from positivist epistemology where validity and reliability are primary. However, practitioner-researchers work from the interpretivist position in which the focus is on trustworthiness and authenticity. Their perspective is that of researchers-in-action. However, 'goodness' criteria in interpretivist research – multiple methods, rigour, attention to detail, transparency – remain central (see Fossey et al, 2002). Insider researcher-practitioners must acknowledge the limits and the advantages of their location, adopt the capacity to step back from their practice, and ensure that they remain within a theoretical frame. Supervision, co-leadership and various recording and monitoring strategies are vitally important to so doing.

Researching a system of which one is a part raises many tricky ethical as well as methodological issues, for example, using archived data in the light of privacy laws, ensuring service users are not disadvantaged or compromised in the service they receive. Very importantly, such projects require support from the organization itself. This might entail permitting a worker to access the clients of other workers, or giving assent to taking the results of 'insider' research seriously, even if it suggests significant changes to the status quo of practice. (For a detailed discussion of these issues and others, see Campbell, 1997).

If the group is an on-going long term group, it will be very important for the researcher-practitioner to identify a time period during which they will observe, monitor and record the group's progress, perhaps repeating the data gathering and observations after several months in order to have comparative data to analyse. With a time limited group, the research or evaluation can be part of the entire 'life' of the group, with some data gathered at strategic points, for example, at the beginning, middle and end when participants might be surveyed or complete standardized tests such as Quality of Life scales. Recording group processes may take place continuously, for example through the use of journals by both leaders and participants.

Where do we go from here?

I have been arguing that it is essential that we increase our efforts to identify groupwork practice as a research location, that is, as a site demanding rigorous attention from researchers on an ongoing basis. There exists a small but useful body of research already but it is somewhat limited both in size and in methodological focus. Being aware of and sensitive to the particularities of groupwork as an intervention and a practice, suggests that we need to be more adventurous in designing research that is multidimensional and multimethod. Research can most usefully come from a combined 'assault' from 'outsider' and 'insider' locations. As we have discussed, different designs and approaches are relevant depending on where the researcher is located and each has an inter-related contribution to make. As an example, it is interesting to read the following two publications as a pair. Kissane et al (2004) conducted a RCT on a group intervention for women with advanced breast cancer. While the final results are not yet available, they report on the process of doing the research, the mixed quantitative and qualitative methods, and reflect on the benefits from the point of view of researchers and therapists providing the intervention. The women who were in the group later spontaneously published their own account (The Thursday Girls,

2004). Taken together, these studies provide a very rich and multi-faceted picture of the impact of the intervention.

We know that there are gaps in what we know about outcome in group interventions. For example:

- We know little about the appropriateness of groupwork in different contexts or cultures, about the importance of characteristics of participants – gender, class, marginalized status, ethnicity – in affecting the way people use or may benefit from groupwork. People from different cultures or minority groups have rarely been studied in relation to group interventions and therefore (until we have the research findings) we should be circumspect in 'importing' group interventions and expecting them to work for everyone
- We know little about the views of consumers on group interventions. Group participants are as yet a largely untapped source with regard to involvement in research

To date we have tended to utilize research designs and approaches that are well-established. There is room for thinking about different designs and approaches. For example, Conversation Analysis (Silverman, 1993) as a method for placing a micro focus on the group as 'talk-in-interaction' may yield interesting insights about the ways in which talk shapes identity, and how groupworkers might use talk more strategically.

Some work has been done on the elements that make group programs 'time-effective' for participants, dissolving the short-term/long-term divide of much group outcome research (McKenzie, 1994; Helfmann, 1994; Piper and Joyce, 1996, Budman, 1996). Identifying 'time-effectiveness' or the 'dose-response curve' for group interventions for people with different issues would seem to offer a very useful contribution to our thinking about the elements in groupwork which make a difference to participants and how quickly or effectively they can be achieved. This suggests a very valuable perspective and research focus to bring to group outcome research.

We need to think more creatively and strategically about how the voices and experiences of group program consumers or participants can be included in the design and analysis of group programs, indeed their potential as co-researchers. We might, for instance, adopt a Participatory Action Research design (Wadsworth, 1997), or design research around the kinds of questions prior group participants propose are the ones they would like answers to. Using prior group participants as a critical reference group to assist in designing, monitoring and interpreting research on groups is another possible strategy.

Very importantly too, we need, as group leaders, to have an openness to learning from the findings of group outcome studies. Such findings should inform our practice, but 'taking them on board' is often quite difficult for practitioners – all of us are potential 'victims' of our own sometimes idiosyncratic beliefs about 'what works' in groupwork. But the research endeavour is incomplete unless it leads to the creation of systematized knowledge, supported by evidence, which is communicated to those who work in the field, who then make use of it.

References

Bloch, S. (1988) Research in group psychotherapy. in M. Aveline and W. Dryden (Eds.) *Group therapy in Britain*. Milton Keynes: Open University Press

Bloch, S., and Aveline, M. (1996) Group psychotherapy. in S. Bloch, S. (Ed) *An introduction to the psychotherapies*. New York: Oxford University Press

Borkovec, T.D. and Miranda, J. (1999) Between-group psychotherapy outcome research and basic science. *Journal of Clinical Psychology*, 55, 2, 147-158

Budman, S.H. (1996) Time-limited group psychotherapy for patients with personality disorders: Outcomes and dropouts. *International Journal of Group Psychotherapy*, 46, 3, 357-377

Campbell, L. (1997) Good and proper: Considering ethics in practice research. *Australian Social Work*, 50, 4, 29-36

Donenberg, G.R. (1999) Reconsidering between-group psychotherapy outcome research and basic science': Applications to child and adolescent psychotherapy outcome research. *Journal of Clinical Psychology*, 55, 2, 181-190

Edmonds, C.V.I., Lockwood, G.A., and Cunningham, A.J. (1999) Psychological response to long term group therapy: A randomized trial with metastatic breast cancer patients. *Journal of PsychoOncology*, 8, 74-91

Fossey, E., Harvey, C., McDermott, F., and Davidson, L. (2002) Understanding and evaluating qualitative research. *RANZ Journal of Psychiatry*, 36, 6, 717-732

Harding, R., and Higginson, I.J. (2003) What is the best way to help caregivers in cancer and palliative care? A systematic literature review of interventions and their effectiveness. *Palliative Medicine*, 17, 63-74

Helfmann, B. (1994) Here is now. *International Journal of Group Psychotherapy*, 44, 4, 429-436

Kanas, N. (2001) Treatment outcome in group therapy. *International Journal of Group Psychotherapy*, 51, 2, 289-291

Kissane, D.W., Grabsch, B. Clarke, D.M., Christie, G., Clifton, D., Gold, S., Hill, C., Morgan, A., McDermott, F., and Smith, G.C. (2004) Supportive-expressive group therapy: The transformation of existential ambivalence into creative living while enhancing adherence to anti-cancer therapies. *Psycho-Oncology*, 13, 11, 755-768

Krause, M.S., and Howard, K.I. (1999) 'Between-group psychotherapy outcome research and basic science' revisited. *Journal of Clinical Psychology*, 55, 2, 159-169

Lewis, C. (2004) 'What works' in groupwork? Towards an ethical framework for measuring effectiveness. Paper presented at the 10th European Groupwork Symposium, York, July

Long, S. (1992 *A structural analysis of small groups*. London: Routledge

McDermott, F. (2002) *Inside Group Work: A guide to reflective practice*. St Leonards, NSW: Allen & Unwin

McDermott, F. (2003) Researching outcome: Group work in mental health. *Australian Social Work*, 56, 4, 352-363

McKenzie, K.R. (1994) Where is here and when is now? The adaptational challenge of mental health reform for group psychotherapy. *International Journal of Group Psychotherapy*, 44, 4, 407-427

McKenzie, K.R. (2001) An expectation of radical changes in the future of group psychotherapy. *International Journal of Group Psychotherapy*, 52, 2, 175-178

McTaggart, R. (1993) Action research: Issues in theory and practice. *Annual Review of Social Sciences*, Geelong: Deakin University

Nietzel, M.T., Russell, R.T., Hemmings, K.A., and Gretter, M.L. (1987) Clinical significance of psychotherapy for unipolar depression: A meta analytic approach to social comparison. *Journal of Consulting and Clinical Psychology*, 55, 2, 156-171

Piper, W.E. and Joyce, A.S. (1996) A consideration of factors influencing the use of time-limited, short-term group therapy. *International Journal of Group Psychotherapy*, 46, 3, 311-327

Pollio, D.E. (2002) The evidence-based group worker. *Social Work with Groups*, 25, 4, 57-70

Preston-Shoot, M. (2004a) 'Evidence: The final frontier?' Star Trek, groupwork and the mission of change. Paper presented at the 10th European Groupwork Symposium, York, July

Preston-Shoot, M. (2004b) 'Evidence: The final frontier?' Star Trek, groupwork and the mission of change. *Groupwork,* 14, 3, 18-43

The Thursday Girls, (2004) *A Life to Live: A group journey with advanced breast cancer.* Carlton NA: PsychOz Publications

Silverman, D. (1993 *Interpreting Qualitative Data: Talk, text and interaction.* London: Sage

Steiner, L., Kjell, P.B., and Hogland, P. (2002) Change during and after long-term analytic group psychotherapy. *International Journal of Group Psychotherapy,*

52, 3, 419-424

Westbury, E., and Tutty, L.M. (1999) The efficacy of group treatment for survivors of childhood abuse. *Child Abuse and Neglect*, 23, 1, 31-44

Wadsworth, Y. (1997) *Everyday Evaluation on the Run*. St.Leonards, NSW: Allen & Unwin

Wilberg, T. and Karterud, S. (2001) The place of group psychotherapy in the treatment of personality disorders. *Current Opinion in Psychiatry*, 14, 2, 125-129

Yalom, I.F. (1975) *The Theory and Practice of Group Psychotherapy*. New York: Basic Books

This chapter first published in 2005 in *Groupwork* Vol. 15(1), pp.90-108

At the time of writing, the author was a Senior Lecturer in the ***School*** of Social Work, The University of Melbourne

Developing critical conversations about practice

Mark Smith

***Abstract**: In this article I examine the place of groups in developing conversation about professional practice. In particular, I focus on 'study groups' involving informal and community educators engaged in initial and in-service education programmes. My interest lies in how we may transcend individualised responses through building 'critical communities of enquirers' (Carr and Kemmis, 1986, p.40). Material is drawn here from a series of taped conversations with participants in study groups - and written recordings of 126 hours of such groups. These formed part of a larger research project (Smith, 1994a; 1994b).*

***keywords:** study groups; recorded interviews; critical conversation; group process*

Collective explorations of practice

Informal and community educators operate on their own initiative for a great deal of the time. Frequently they have to make difficult choices concerning their actions and deal with distressing situations. Not surprisingly, many have sought forums where they can talk about or explore practice. One expression of this has been the tradition of supervision (see, for example Tash, 1967; Kadushin, 1992). Another involves talking informally with peers. Such talk is a means of counteracting the isolation that many feel; marking the membership of the occupational group; and a mechanism of social control. Yet, as Pithouse (1987) has shown in respect of social workers, such relationships are carefully managed. Informal consultancies usually exist on the basis of friendship and commonality of role or experience - and exchanges are typically privatised and covert. A more public forum around policy has been provided by trade unions and professional associations.

Open, grounded, and collective exploration of practice does not take place on any substantial scale. As one practitioner put it:

> One of the things I think is missing is a sense of unity with other workers - and we haven't got that because we don't really talk about the work. Things aren't really public.

The nearest that many practitioners come to it is in the discussion of particular cases, clients or groups. Here, however, the focus is on the issues and questions that arise in relation to, for example, the dynamics of a particular family or group. What workers are actually thinking and feeling in their day to day conversations with individuals and group members - and how this fits with some common purpose - are secondary concerns.

Privatising reflection on work is not simply the product of established norms and trade-offs, and fears around exploring practice. The intellectual traditions that infuse practice have also fed a failure to develop understandings which locate people's lived experiences. Here I want to pick up on three connected strands. First, much of the current literature concerning groups and supervision draws heavily on psycho-dynamic insights and metaphors. This can be contrasted with earlier social groupwork practitioners such as Coyle (1930) who drew heavily on pragmatism and on educational discourses (see, for example, Reid, 1981, pp.103-136). Many of those writing still 'tend to slip past structure to focus on isolated situations' and to consider problems as 'the problems of individuals' (Mills, 1943, p.534). We need to work to hold onto an appreciation of the shifting relationships and imbalances in which our work is located.

Second, and historically linked to this, is the extent to which western discourses are populated by a one-sided appreciation of selfhood. Individuals are seen as self-contained and unitary. They 'carry their uniqueness deep inside themselves, like pearls hidden in their shells' (Burkitt, 1991, p.1). The result is a tendency to appeal to what supposedly goes on inside us, rather than to the interactions between us and the environment in which they take place. Not only is there a sense of the individual as a bounded container, separated from other containers, but each is seen as in 'possessionship or ownership of its own capacities and abilities' (Sampson, 1993, p.31). Such views of selfhood - and their focus on the unconscious - are culturally and historically specific (Cohen, 1994); and gendered in the way that the self becomes 'embodied' (Moore, 1994).

Third, writers such as Grundy (1987) have made clear our long-standing attachment to what Habermas (1972) describes as technical rather than emancipatory interests. Our activities as practitioners do not exist in a vacuum. They are produced and experienced in specific social and historical conditions - and involve particular moral and political considerations. We, therefore, need to cultivate a consciousness in our activities of the kind of future we hope to build. What we engage in is 'intrinsically political, affecting the life chances of those involved in the process by affecting their access to an interesting life and material well-being' (Carr and Kemmis, 1986, p.39).

Such matters can only be addressed as both personal and collective concerns. Judgements about what makes for the good, for human flourishing, have to be both individual and shared. If we individually decide what is right without reference to the wishes and views of others then we are succumbing to ways of working which are self-serving, anti-dialogical, and designed to subordinate rather than emancipate. The cultivation of judgement is dependent upon forms of communal life that facilitate engagement and conversation about what makes for the good (Bernstein, 1983, p.225). Here we see the makings of a powerful case for collective explorations of practice. They provide us with a rationale for looking at not just at what we may be feeling or thinking, but also at our interactions, and how these may be located within a dialogue about what may be appropriate for a particular community of practice such as informal education.

The mechanics of study groups

Study groups are an attempt to bring the exploration of practice and the generation of a community of practice to the fore. Their mechanics are straightforward. Agreed periods of time are allocated for the exploration of a specific encounter or intervention (around 45-60 minutes per person). The practitioner involved begins by presenting verbally an outline of the intervention. One of the rules often made by these groups is that 'presenters' should also provide a short written summary containing the main points or a recording. The group then works with this material. One briefing for those involved in initial training suggests the aim is to explore:

1. what was happening in the particular encounter;
2. what alternatives were possible; and
3. what knowledge and skills were being used and the ones that could have been used, and to identify those feelings and attitudes that were promoting or hindering the task (YMCA George Williams College, 1994).

Participants are encouraged to focus on what people do - the actual interventions they make - not on what they would like to do; and to work on the material presented, not on the worker. From such an exploration of practice, they may then move on to more general thinking about the particular area of work. It is an important tenet of such groups that it is not the presenter alone who is learning from the presentation. As group members work to help the person to clarify and refine their understandings, they also enhance their own learning and enlarge their abilities to engage in dialogue (Jeffs and Smith, 1990, p.10).

Before sessions begin groups usually set out basic rules of conduct and then review these as they go. Often sessions are structured so that there is time for at least two presentations/explorations and a space for drawing out general themes and questions (without going back over the specifics of the presentations).

Exploring practice collectively: Key dimensions of the experience

One way of making sense of this process is derived from supervision. The focus is on the practice of an individual, but instead of there being a single supervisor, the group collectively scrutinises the work. Indeed some writers describe this process as group supervision (Hawkins and Shohet (1989, pp.95-117). However, unlike supervision, a primary concern is the learning of the whole group, not just the understanding of the individual whose practice provides the focus. This links back to earlier concerns expressed about an over-concentration on pyschodynamic models. For the process to work, individual practitioners must share what they have decided to do with a particular individual or group, why that decision was made, how the decision was carried out and what the outcome was. They need also to bring their own person into the situation, describing the processes of their own 'mind and heart'.

Much of the success of these group explorations of practice lies in the way participants get hold of basic tenets and mould them. What is also of particular interest is the extent to which these 'rules' or dimensions mirror key aspects of their practice as educators.

Focusing on the work rather than the person of the worker

One, central, tenet is that it is the work that is the centre of attention rather than the character of the worker. As one participant put it, 'we separated the deed from the person'. This was not without difficulty:

> People say it is not a personal thing, it is just about work, I can't separate the work from the personal thing, because I think the work is personal in a way... It is like going to the dentist. I think your work is part of you.

This entwining of personal and professional identities involves a double paradox for workers. 'The personal rewards to be found in their work come only from self-investment in it and ..., when the cost of the latter is too high, the rewards are also reduced' (Nias, 1989, p.18). Separating the worth of the person from the deed and, in turn, recognising the limits of any such split, helps us to approach questions of personal investment - and takes us back to questions of ownership. Here, we examine what happened and that necessarily involves questions about who and what we are. While it remains a risky business, it is, at least, constrained by the focus on the work: the central question concerns the appropriateness of our actions as workers - as members of a community of practice - not whether we are 'nice' people to know. This can inhibit direct attacks on the person, but the process can still be painful:

> However open minded you might present yourself, it is difficult to accept criticism that lightly. Even when you are prepared to accept it is still quite a challenging experience.

Clearly, what we do in a situation has to be owned by us. However, we must act in situations where there is much that we cannot know; where the tools we employ are necessarily tentative; where communication is stuttering and partial; and where there are always a number of different, and often conflicting, paths we can take. Practice will always be imperfect; it will always be problematic. We will always have something to learn. Once we recognise that fallibility is a part and parcel of working, and that such groups are opportunities to learn from our mistakes, then the task becomes a little more manageable.

Being prepared to challenge and to accept challenge

Given recognition of fallibility, and concern not to attack people (and not be attacked ourselves), groups have the potential to be cosy. They can be 'too nice, too comfortable' and 'padded for comfort'. Part of the task may be to work for a more exploratory or challenging environment:

> I knew it would benefit me, so I wanted to get what I could get out it. I was wanting more understanding. I wanted to know why I wasn't happy with this. I wanted to learn from it. I have got an all-absorbing thing about

learning. You can get analysis paralysis, so that is why it is refreshing to get other people questioning your work.

Fears remain around the discomfort and disruption that can be involved. Much of the way the process is experienced depends on the initial frame of reference or orientation of participants:

> The pieces of work I brought were extremely important to me. I thought this is my time, I am going to use it. I was in a positive frame of mind... Another thing was the respect of your colleagues. Sometimes somebody would ask something that made me go 'Ouch!', but I would respect them for that.

This is a significant response. First, there is the question of ownership - the practitioner talks about 'my time' rather than 'our time'. He appears to be using a metaphor from individual supervision and is falling into the trap outlined earlier. Second, he interprets the challenging occurring in the group as part of a professional discourse. Being asked questions in this way, engaging in this process, signified entry into, or a place in, that discourse - he was 'being professional'.

Exploring practitioner processes, rather than the 'client' or what to do next

Another dimension of these groups is the way in which the focus is kept on what happened: what the person was thinking and feeling in the situation, what did they do, what were the natures of the interactions and so on? Giving advice or handy hints was not what was required:

> The positive thing is focusing on a specific thing and not making it too general and getting other people's opinion on the intervention. Why certain things had happened, what had you done to create the situation. I don't like getting into the bits where people say 'if that had been me I would have done this', that wasn't you and you didn't do it.

The focus is on practitioner processes. It is an exploration of praxis (informed, committed action):

> Quite often I found that many of the problems were not with the young people or with the group or the piece of work, but rather with yourself - with your own confidence or maybe assertion of when was it your right to intervene.

The group is not there to make speculative guesses or interpretations concerning the other person or people, but to examine the worker's thinking and action so that all may learn. Where participants avoid doing this, or are still learning to focus on an actual moment in their practice (an intervention), then there are tensions:

> I sense being blocked by other presenters at times and then you think it is totally useless being involved in this because he or she won't let you have a look... The job is not able to be done. The work is not looked at.

The briefings given to group members were fairly explicit in relation to focus and it was often a matter for some discussion in the groups in the contract setting phase.

Holding boundaries

Considerable attention tends to be paid to establishing and holding boundaries - especially in relation to task. Two further boundaries were named by participants in conversation as important. First, time: explorations tend to last their contracted time and no more. This is to ensure that each member of the group has their fair share of time. Second, 'confidentiality' is nearly always an important element of the initial contract:

> The boundaries were fairly clear, particularly around confidentiality. My feeling is that if people do not understand that 100 per cent then there are grave risks. The idea is that it is the opportunity to explore what you are doing. In that situation it may well come out that you hate your boss or whatever it is and you have to be safe enough to say that. It is one of those situations where the safety and the risk need to balance.

Attending to group process

For such groups to work effectively it is necessary for participants to pay attention to the way they are functioning as individuals and the totality of the interactions. This area can be a major source of learning for many participants:

> It took me a while to learn how to function in a group. To not be the centre of attention all the time. The intervention may be around whoever, but for me I was still the focus of attention. It took me quite a while to come to grips with that, accept it, and learn to be a member of a group so that I could actually help somebody.

Part of this movement involves a shift from experiencing the group as a context for interaction. Instead the group becomes an instrument 'where the group members are able to work as a unit to explore and exploit the resources that the group contains or to which it has access' (Douglas, 1993, p.31).

Group members may be aware of dealing with people in different ways, although not always knowing why:

> Some members I will ask more willingly. It is mostly about their vulnerability although there is one member of the group that I like having a go at. I do it jokey. I don't understand that relationship.

Others struggle against this:

> I consciously tried to not treat anybody differently because I liked them better than anyone else - because you always do in life. I wanted to give everyone equal value for money. Part of the group maintenance bit was that people did play the game. You felt you wanted to give the person presenting a fair deal, to enable them to get the most out of the thing.

Some groups were conducted over a short intensive period such as a residential. Others were conducted monthly over a period of three years:

> When the study group works together for a long time, things merge and everybody contributes and stuff becomes communal property. You develop ways of working together.

For those in long-term groups, reflection on the changes and developments is a crucial aspect of the experience for some participants. One of the indicators of the relative maturity of the group used by participants is the extent to which barriers come down and it is possible to work on sensitive material: 'It is getting more intimate, to the nitty gritty'. This simultaneous or parallel attention to the process of the group and to the material presented is one of the hallmarks of these groups. As things progress, members are often able to flip between the two and to use understandings about one to inform the other (see below).

Preparation, follow-up and the use of recordings

Participants need to identify a piece of work that has enough material for the group to work on. In addition, a number of 'presenters' want to identify key questions beforehand so that they have some focus for learning and exploration. Some take possible situations and questions to individual supervision. Others prefer not to:

> Often I used to think 'why didn't I do so and so' just by writing it down. Then I used to get so much out of the groups that I think I wouldn't have wanted to spoil it in supervision. It would have taken something away. I quite liked the ducking and diving.

There are problems when presenters come over-prepared: where they had either over-worked the piece and had grown tired with it; or where they are nervous about the experience and try to work out the various angles beforehand. Given the vulnerability that many experience such a response is not surprising. However, it can stimulate a particular reaction:

> I sometimes used to get the impression that people used to bring a piece of work that they already had the answers for. No matter what anyone said that piece of work was history or placed in a compartment with 'solved' printed on it.

This was a theme that emerged regularly in the conversations. Once people made a commitment to engage with their and others' practice, then attempts to avoid the subject were seen as undermining.

For presenters the experience of the workshops or groups can be intense, especially where they bring substantial material and want to work in the group on it: 'there were so many things coming thick and fast, trying to recall all those different things was difficult'. Concerns such as this led some workers to emphasise follow-up work. This typically involves recording their experiences after the group - and reflecting on them in supervision.

Being a facilitator

The task of the facilitator in this setting - as with any other form of humanistic groupwork - is to effect two complementary objectives. 'The first is the development of the democratic mutual aid system; the second is the actualisation of purpose' (Glassman and Kates, 1990, p.105; see also Mullender and Ward, 1991). Inevitably, we are drawn to the significant role played by the groupworker in establishing or helping to adapt the group so that work of this kind can take place. Here the two 'complementary objectives' can be represented as :

1. Establishing the task: facilitators have to work with the group to establish a clear understanding of the task. While there may be an initial written briefing, there are inevitably questions concerning the exact framing of the task. Beyond this, facilitators establish the

task by engaging in it - by asking questions of presenters, exploring themes and issues. Last, they are also likely, from time to time, to have to remind people of the focus of the discussion.

2. Establishing boundaries: here a common approach is to open a discussion early on concerning the ways in which the group can work, and what agreements should be concerning confidentiality, time, relationships and procedure. As the group operates, facilitators then have some responsibility for encouraging the review of these matters.

Once the framework for the conduct of the groups is established and worked at over a period, interventions made by facilitators change but we should not overlook the extent to which they remain a major resource for the group (Douglas, 1993, p.95). Their position in relation to the group allows them to approach questions with regard to activity, interaction and sentiment (Homans, 1951, pp.33-40) with a different set of constraints to that enjoyed by the others involved. Facilitators are participants (perhaps providing one model for engaging with the material), but there is often also an expectation that they will approach questions of process, functioning and the extent to which the group is contributing to human wellbeing. Of course, as the group becomes more 'self-directed' these matters will also be owned by members - but two dimensions of facilitators were noted by participants in conversation. First, they are seen as possessing repertoires of routines, examples and experiences that can benefit the group. Second, and crucially, they are in a position to make use of these. In this sense they may be perceived as 'longstops'.

The framework established at the start with the group appears to enable people to take responsibility. In conversation, participants emphasise the high degree of involvement in the process; wholly non-participating group members are relatively rare. If group members begin to recognise a consistent pattern of non-involvement then this frequently becomes the subject of conversation in the reflective/evaluative sessions that follow the examination of individual's work. The 'longstop' role assumes particular significance in situations where there are other, continuing relationships or a history of interaction. The most obvious example here is when seeking to work in this way with teams of practitioners or with units (i.e. involving clients, workers, managers and so on). Here, having someone outside the situation or the established relationships to facilitate process, and bring to the notice of the group questions concerning, for example, deviations from the task or the agreed boundaries, can be valued. There is also something about having someone involved who has 'a safe pair of hands'. The process holds a number of risks and a facilitator provides something of a safety net.

Many of the participants I had conversations with had worked with a number of different facilitators and thus were able to compare styles and approaches. This is a not untypical response:

> The most useful approach has been when the facilitator has challenged, but has thrown it back at the group or the individual. Rather than challenging someone and saying 'what about this?' or whatever, taking it from their (the facilitator's) point of view. Personally I haven't found that as useful. At the end of the day it is about the group's learning and individuals within that group... It might be about saying 'you are not challenging this person', 'look at what you are doing within the group' or 'this is not taking place as it should, that is not an intervention'. Getting people to look actually at the piece of work. It is quite easy to drift into the easy way out.

A significant feature of this latter response is that it is also what is expected from other participants. That is to say, all participants are expected to take responsibility for their own learning and to simultaneously work with material in such a way as to allow others to create frameworks and come to appreciations for themselves.

The impact of study groups

In looking at what participants said about the experience of exploring practice in study groups we have already had some strong indicators of what they gain. Here I pick up dimensions that appeared with some frequency in conversations.

Developing practitioner identities

One of the strongest and most consistent themes was the extent to which repeated and thorough explorations of practice helped to build people's confidence in themselves as particular kinds of practitioners. Through the group explorations, and linking in with supervision, self reflection, reading and informal discussions with peers, a picture emerges of what a 'good' practitioner might be. Through exploring practice, participants can recognise their abilities in such a way as to be able fully to take on an occupational identity. More specifically, for many, their experience of sustained exploration of practice in a public way with peers, and a recognition of their capacities in this area, can cement an understanding of themselves as professional (two workers speaking):

> We were talking about professional detachment and I think these were very much part of the process of gaining that detachment. You can cut yourself off from the process and look at it objectively. Spend time reflecting, analysing, deciding on action.

> Common themes seem to come out. I think that was the thing that made you feel part of the profession. What was being said or professed, you are professing some knowledge of them, was things that you could really relate to.

It is a process that can be enhanced by having a comprehensive environment in which practice and identity could be explored. By being able to tack between supervision, peer exploration, individual reflection, workers can realise change:

> This time last year I had major problems with my identity as a worker. I was struggling with the project work but fighting against being an informal educator. It was going back to supervision and starting again... It suddenly dawned on me what I had heard other people saying. You have got to let the group decide for themselves and take their own decisions. You sit and watch workers and think they are not doing anything, but then you realise they are. They are taking the back seat. It was working out all my biases about the way that other workers had worked.

Listening, observing, asking questions

The act of engaging with material in the sessions, and subsequent reflection and study of that experience, allows for the honing of dialogical abilities. For example, recognising that others are competent and that you can listen and observe while participating:

> An ability to listen to other people and to try and understand where they are coming from. At times to not actively take part, but to sit back and see a process happening. That I found quite fascinating. Especially where you can see where one person is going and what the other person is struggling for. At times you could see the enlightenment come, the understanding. Sitting back, and even though you could understand what the questioner was trying to get across, to sit back and watch that happen. Not interfere because they had the ability to do it, so it was an acceptance that other people have the expertise.

There was also the development of the ability to question material: to make interpretations and judgements:

> As a participant it is also about learning how to question stuff... As time progressed it was much easier to question and not offer solutions. That has taught me things about working with people in general. In particular, about how you judge stuff. The judgement I make is based on what people say to me. I need to check that out and by questioning in an appropriate manner and not by challenging in terms of the person or the personality. It is about what is actually being done, not about the individual who is doing it.

These abilities were not confined to the forum of the study group. They could be used and developed in other settings: for engaging in meetings and for thinking about one's own processes.

Generating frameworks for practice

Enhancing the ability to make judgements and interpretations, and to ask questions, involves the development of practitioner frames of reference. As the groups developed so too did these frameworks:

> They helped me to get a framework to analyse things. You read and think about different ideas... Suddenly you have this coathanger to hang on how we analyse certain situations. It was just like everybody else's experiences coming in. Then you realise 'Oh I never thought of it like that...'

One of the significant features of these frameworks is that they are both individual and shared:

> We are beginning to get a structure for questions - aims, what is your role, how do you think the other people saw you, what do think they saw their role as, what were you feeling, we seem to go through a set of questions. I don't know how it happened - it just developed.

Individuals can sit down and analyse a piece of work along these dimensions. Similarly, they might be used as they reflect-in-action, as an element of internal supervision. At the same time if we analyse the processes of groups that have been working together for some time, then these frameworks become revealed in the nature and direction of the questioning.

Two further dimensions concerning this emerging framework were particularly noticeable when reviewing the conversations I had with participants. These are the importance of staying in touch with feelings; and of owning ideas, feeling and actions:

> It made me recognise... how many people weren't admitting how they were feeling at the time of what they were doing. I realised that if I am going to learn I will have to unblock that and say this is how I am feeling and I felt that at the time.

A significant proportion of questions asked, and statements made in groups concern the feelings of the presenter (and, indeed, those of the participants). Such statements tend to be increasingly prefaced by statements such as 'I think'. That is to say that they were not thrown in as abstract or unattributed statements that could be passed off onto others, but were owned by the individuals. They were grounded in an appreciation of practice.

The way in which practitioners develop and make use of theory can also be revealed through looking and relooking at the process of the groups. What occurs is that statements are made and questions are asked about a particular piece of work, an intervention made by a worker. Through this process, the tacit and often unacknowledged theories and ideas that guide the way we respond to situations, our theory-in-use (Argyris and Schön, 1977) can be exposed and interrogated. We might contrast them with our espoused theory (what we say we are doing when asked) or with other theories or propositions. This form of exploring the theories that practitioners use enables the development of grounded understandings. If practice is understood as praxis informed, committed action - we are able to get beyond the idea that theory and practice are mutually exclusive realms; that, for example, practice is developed when we apply theory. Practice cannot exist without theory, nor can it be separated from questions of value and disposition. It is precisely this that becomes revealed in the process of the groups.

Expanding practitioners' repertoires

In addition to developing practitioners' central appreciative systems, these groups also allow people to add to their store of images, ideas and examples: their repertoire (Schön, 1983). 'You add to that reservoir of knowledge. You are developing a bank of knowledge'. This consists not so much of concrete examples that can be mechanically applied, as of metaphors or starting points. This disparate collection of metaphors can be worked with. It is this 'working with' which, arguably, constitutes 'good practice'.

Understanding group processes and being able to work collectively

One outcome that appears with some regularity in conversations with participants concerns the way in which reflection on the experience enhanced people's understandings of group processes in general, and cultivated an ability to work collectively. The intensity of the experience and the anxieties involved around the exploration of one's own work created a rich store of material for reflection:

> As a participant observer, it brought it home to you. Being involved in that group helped you to grasp... the way you worked within the group. How you responded to other people, what roles you took on, how your role changed depending on who was in the spotlight or whatever. All those things were learning from being part of the group.

Individuals can also develop an ability to draw attention to the process of the group, what is happening in the immediate situation, and to use this to further understanding. Examples here include comments on the presenter's emotional state or comment on the impact of the presentation on the group. This is a fundamental move that can occur as groups mature. It involves grasping the possibility of people 'when recounting or exploring a previous experience or relationship' to relive aspects or transfer elements into the current situation. There are three dimensions to this. A focus on whatever is being carried by the presenter, both consciously and unconsciously from the intervention (what some would describe as counter-transference); a focus on the 'here-and-now process as a mirror or parallel of the there-and-then-process' (Hawkins and Shohet, 1989, p.58); and a focus on participants' own experience in the group. That is to say the feelings, thoughts and images the material stirs up in them and how these can be used for learning in the group (ibid, p.58). Here we are able to draw upon a rich vein of metaphors and ideas from psychodynamic theorising. A significant element in this 'drawing upon' is that it takes place here within a social groupwork framework and as such also draws on contrasting traditions of practice. Most significant here is the 'explicit development of a democratic group form in conjunction with the actualisation of group purpose (Glassman and Kates, 1990, p.110).

Lastly, the process of groups can be used in other settings e.g. to develop teams with whom participants are working. Here, there can be some difficulties because they involve a range of relationships and experiences that have to be acknowledged and worked with e.g. workers are exploring their practice with managers and vice versa. The interventions brought may already be known to other participants. This can bring a special problem in that they begin to work with their memory of the situation rather than the account of the relationships and processes furnished by the presenter (Christian and Kitto, 1987). However, what the group can help develop is an expanded vocabulary for describing and exploring work within the team. It can help members to appreciate how others work. And the experience of working in this way within one arena can impact upon collective work undertaken elsewhere, for example, in full team meetings.

In conclusion: developing a critical community of practice

There are a number of overlapping reasons why we should seek to encourage and participate in the critical and collective enquiry into practice. The judgements we make are not simply matters of individual choice but must involve dialogue with others. This is both because we are dealing with matters of human well-being and because understanding itself is achieved through dialogue. Moreover, through our engagement with such communities and groupings we develop and sustain our identity as practitioners. We also directly develop our understanding and appreciation of the processes and projects that lie at the heart of our work. What emerges is a shared framework for thinking about things.

These concerns are obviously linked to a wish to further the democratic project and ideas about the worth of each and every person. The process of participating in study groups helps practitioners not only to articulate what they are doing to each other, but also to those they are working with and to the public at large. As such they are a contribution to a more open and democratic occupation or community of practice; and they help deepen public accountability. Furthermore, participation in such groups provides practitioners with models for democratic engagement in other areas of their work.

There are also considerable gains from this form of engagement for theorising within and across different communities of practice. A good example here has been the tendency within youth work in recent years to turn to paradigms and practices in parallel occupations rather than to interrogate the traditions of actual practice that have emerged (Smith, 1988). Explorations of interventions and situations in the ways discussed here allow for the generation of grounded theory and ways of making sense that more closely connect with the concerns and actions of workers in different areas. In turn, these can also be used to deepen discussion across occupational boundaries.

Collective explorations of practice hold great potential. Their power does not lie in some simple notion that by having more people look at something you create the possibility of knowing more. It connects with something fundamental about practice. Practice is a social process involving ideas about what makes for the good. As such it is lost without collective exploration.

References

Argyris, C. and Schön, D. (1977) *Theory into Practice. Increasing Professional Effectiveness.* San Francisco: Jossey-Bass.

Bernstein, R.J. (1983) *Beyond Objectivism and Relativism. Science, Hermeneutics and Praxis.* Oxford: Blackwell.

Burkitt, I. (1991) *Social Selves. Theories of the Social Formation of Personality.* London: Sage.

Carr, W. and Kemmis, S. (1986) *Becoming Critical: Education, Knowledge and Action Research.* Lewes: Falmer.

Christian, C. and Kitto, J. (1987) *The Theory and Practice of Supervision.* London: YMCA National College.

Cohen, A.P. (1994) *Self Consciousness: An Alternative Anthropology of Identity.* London: Routledge.

Coyle, G. (1930) *Social Process in Organized Groups.* New York: Richard R. Smith.

Douglas, T. (1993) *A Theory of Groupwork Practice.* London: Macmillan.

Glassman, U. and Kates, L. (1990) *Group Work: A Humanistic Approach.* Newbury Park: Sage.

Grundy, S. (1987) *Curriculum: Product or Praxis.* Lewes: Falmer.

Habermas, J. (1972) *Knowledge and Human Interests.* (Trans. J. J. Shapiro). London: Heinemann.

Hawkins, P. and Shohet, R. (1989) *Supervision in the Helping Professions: An Individual, Group and Organizational Approach.* Milton Keynes: Open University Press.

Homans, G. (1951) *The Human Group.* London: Routledge and Kegan Paul.

Jeffs, T. and Smith, M. (eds.) (1990) *Using Informal Education: An Alternative to Casework, Teaching and Control?* Buckingham: Open University Press.

Kadushin, A. (1992) *Supervision in Social Work.* New York: Columbia University Press.

Mills, C.W. (1943) 'The professional ideology of social pathologists', *American Journal of Sociology*, 49(2) and reprinted in Horowitz, I.L. (ed.) (1963) *Power, Politics and People: The Collected Essays of C. Wright Mills.* New York: Oxford University Press.

Moore, H. (1994) *A Passion for Difference: Essays in Anthropology and Gender.* Cambridge: Polity.

Mullender, A. and Ward, D. (1991) *Self-Directed Groupwork. Users Take Action for Empowerment.* London: Whiting & Birch Ltd.

Nias, J. (1989) *Primary Teachers Talking: A Study of Teaching as Work.* London: Routledge.

Pithouse, A. (1987) *Social Work: The Social Organisation of an Invisible Trade.* Aldershot: Avebury.

Reid, K.E. (1981) *From Character Building to Social Treatment: The History of the Use of Groups in Social Work.* Westport: Greenwood Press.

Sampson, E.E. (1993) *Celebrating the Other: A Dialogical Account of Human Nature.* Hemel Hempstead: Harvester Wheatsheaf.

Schön, D. (1983) *The Reflective Practitioner: How Professionals Think in Action.* London: Temple Smith.

Smith, M. (1988) *Developing Youth Work: Informal Education, Mutual Aid and Popular Practice.* Milton Keynes: Open University Press.

Smith, M.K. (1994a) *Local Education: Community, Conversation, Praxis.* Buckingham: Open University Press.

Smith, M.K. (1994b) *Local Education: Some Notes on Method.* Mimeo paper available from author.

Tash, J. (1967) *Supervision in Youth Work: The Report of a Two-Year Training Project in Which Selected Youth Workers Acquired Skills in Supervising.* London: London Council of Social Service.

YMCA George Williams College (1994) *Briefing for Study Groups.* Mimeo.

This chapter first published in 1995 in *Groupwork* Vol. 8(2), pp.134-151

At the time of writing, the author was Rank Research Fellow at the YMCA George Williams College, London

Focus groups and familiar social work skills: Their contribution to practitioner research

Pat Walton

Abstract: *This paper explores the common ground between social work practice with families and groups and practitioner research which uses a qualitative methodology. In particular the author discusses skills which are relevant both to direct practice with families and groups and to collecting research data. The study highlighted in the paper, which concerned the impact on mothers of their children being sexually abused, used a Focus Group as the method of data collection. In exploring the skills relevant to both social work practice and practitioner research the paper discusses the knowledge and values which underpin them. It highlights the shift in power over recent years inherent in worker/service user relationships and suggests that similar issues of power and control need to be addressed when planning and carrying out qualitative research, in particular that which relates to sensitive topics.*

Written from the perspective of a practitioner researcher registered on a post graduate programme, the author suggests that carrying out practitioner research involving service users is important in that it informs both practitioners' own practice and agency policies and procedures.

keywords: *qualitative methodology; focus groups; service users; practitioner research*

Introduction

'Research conducted by practitioners is an idea whose time has come', is the opening sentence of Fuller and Petch's (1995) text on practitioner research. The authors continue by establishing why practitioners should carry out research and how they might acquire the skills to do so. This paper explores some of the knowledge and skills underpinned by a clear value base which trained social workers already have and on which they may draw when considering embarking on research - in particular when collecting information or research data involving service users.

The aim of this paper is to encourage social workers, particularly those involved in child and family work, to consider carrying out research with service users. This will have the potential to both inform their own practice and to lead to agency procedures based on a more meaningful dialogue with children and families.

Professional values, skills and knowledge

In setting up the new national post qualifying professional development framework for child care social workers, CCETSW (1994) prescribes the essential elements of professional competency; these relate to values, skills and knowledge. This paper begins by exploring some of these interlocking elements of social work practice, in particular those which are also relevant when carrying out practitioner research; it then applies these competences to the planning and collecting of data for a small scale qualitative study relating to mothers of children who have been sexually abused.

Whichever activity the professional is attempting, practice or practitioner research, the professional values underpinning the task should remain constant. It is this value base which influences fundamentally the skills inherent in social work practice and in practitioner research. It is appropriate therefore to clarify these values and the evolving knowledge which has informed them over recent years before embarking on an exploration of knowledge and skills which are relevant to current social work practice and to practitioner research.

Values

During the past decade I would argue that there has been a steady move towards a greater sharing of information and power with service users. This requirement to empower service users has had a fundamental effect on social work practice and skills in the field of child protection work and associated family casework and groupwork. It will be noted later that this trend is echoed also in practitioner research.

This shift has been underpinned by several factors - importantly major child care legislation formulated in the wake of a series of public inquiries during the late 1980s relating to the deaths and sexual abuse of children by their carers. The 1989 Children Act and subsequent Department of Health Guidelines (1989) reinforced the duty of statutory agencies to work in partnership with families and children in a greater effort to ensure that wherever possible children are brought up in their own families. To support this philosophy, assessments and clear working contracts involving children, their carers and child protection professionals now have to be drawn up and families have to be invited to case conferences, the major decision making forum in relation to risk to children. All parties are now legally represented in the civil court if a local authority decides to apply for an order because it feels a multi- agency assessment indicates this is necessary in order to protect children. Applications for such orders now have to explain in detail why this degree of intrusion into people's lives is necessary and how this power, if given by the court, will be used. Additionally, complaints procedures and access to files procedures for service users were established by statutory agencies during the late 1980s/early 1990s.

Among other factors influencing this important shift in professional values and practice which relate to the empowerment of service users has been the increasing awareness raising encouraged by the Women's Movement in the 1970s in relation to anti oppressive and anti discriminatory practices. Initially this related to gender issues, in particular the ways in which women both in the family and in the field of employment were oppressed and suffered discrimination. Equal opportunities and anti-discrimination legislation has been passed in relation to gender, as well as in relation to race, disability and sexuality. Much still needs to be done in this respect, not least in relation to ensuring that children's rights are safeguarded (Brannen and O'Brien, 1996).

The training of social workers and other professionals, particularly those involved in child protection work, reflects this awareness raising and increased knowledge in that it is informed by changes both in the values and in the skills which underpin social work practice. These important issues are now central in the training of social workers on basic qualifying courses and, for those who have been in practice for a number of years, agency and post graduate training seek to ensure that their practice is equally well informed.

These values were of central importance in my search for a research methodology. The ways in which they influenced the planning and carrying out of the research will be discussed later in this paper, following consideration of social work skills and knowledge which are based on these values and which are also relevant to practitioner research.

Skills and knowledge

Before exploring the research methodology eventually chosen, in particular the skills required to manage a focus group which was the data collection method adopted, it is appropriate to discuss how more familiar social work knowledge and skills led me to decide that I had the ability to attempt this way of working with research participants. In continuing this discussion, I shall draw on knowledge of groupwork training, and experience of running groups, as well as on systems theory and skills based on it. Knowledge and skills in both areas of work are useful when thinking about and carrying out practitioner research. It is appropriate to emphasise that my practice experience has been gained within statutory settings where the issues of power and control present many challenges for workers and service users.

Brown (1994) offers a classification of groupwork ranging from individual support and maintenance to groupwork which attempts to influence group members' social environment. Inherent in the group's aims is change at an individual and/or at a social level. Change is achieved by the leader intervening in or guiding the group process. Douglas (1978, p.106) discusses the importance of the use of the group process rather than the content in achieving individual change i.e. the interaction of group members rather than what they are saying:

> If we would understand group processes, then we should pay less attention to the speaker and much more to everyone else. The reactions of the others will demonstrate what is happening in the group and that is the primary goal of understanding of anyone who would work with groups.

Heap (1988, p.18) discusses the importance of the group process in bringing about change for the group members and sees the group leader's task as being 'to facilitate, to stimulate and to mobilise the resources inherent in the group process'. Douglas (1978, p.107) refers to the 'management' and 'control' tasks inherent in the role of the group leader. Central to these tasks are observational skills and communication skills.

The ways in which change occurs, importantly who takes responsibility for bringing it about - the group leader, the group or both - depends on various factors. In addition to the social worker's training, the agency which employs her will inevitably influence practice with groups and with families. These influences will relate to the formation and aims of the group as well as important practical issues such as where it will meet and transport/child care arrangements for participants and their children. These factors dictate who will attend the group and for how long groups will run. These decisions are affected fundamentally by economic factors such as central government cuts in public spending.

The focus of social work with groups (and families) in a statutory agency is on helping the individual to change in relation to her/his social functioning at a family level or at the level of interaction with the community (e.g. peer group/school/workplace) because there are issues of risk involved which are in some way related to that behaviour. The women who participated in my research had been members of a group organised by a social services department for mothers involved in statutory child protection procedures because their children had been sexually abused. An important aim of the agency and therefore the group workers had been to help these mothers to cope with the stress they were experiencing in order that they could continue to care for and heal their children (including their children who had not been abused). Central to this task was that of informing and empowering the mothers in order that they would protect their children from further assault from the male abuser/family member. These aims were realised as a result of the women gaining information, increased self confidence and esteem by means of both the group process and the planned interventions of the group leaders. These interventions were within a context of an awareness of the short term nature of the group, given externally imposed time constraints as noted above.

Brown (1994, p.8) notes the increasing additional aims of current groupwork in some settings towards group action and influence:

> Contemporary groupwork emphasises action and influence as well as reaction and adaptation...groupwork provides a context in which individuals help each other; it is a method of helping groups as well as helping individuals (p.8).

Mullender and Ward (1991) highlight the ways in which 'user led analysis' and 'user led action' (p.11) work better in groups. They stress the importance of the group members' interaction in validating individual feelings and experiences and in building on each others skills and strengths not only to cope with but to challenge 'public disinterest or even worse, moral condemnation' (p.12). Collectively group members can identify what needs to change for themselves and can work out strategies to achieve those changes. Butler and Wintram (1991) have stressed the importance of working with groups of women to facilitate their working together collectively in order to build on each other's strengths and to bring about change which is individually and collectively beneficial.

Of major importance in these contemporary group work approaches is the greater sharing of power between group workers and group participants. As already discussed, this philosophy and value base has echoes in recent developments in social work practice in relation to working with families.

These ways of working with service users with the aim of empowering them in order that they may take a greater part in bringing about positive change for themselves and their families, require social workers to have skills based on an ability both to communicate openly and effectively and to formulate with service users clear aims and objectives in relation to their work. Finding common aims and objectives with service users, particularly in the field of child protection work, is sometimes difficult. Social workers need to have the stamina to adhere to empowering ways of working and to the value base which underpins them however challenging this may be.

Further knowledge and intervention skills based on it which are useful to social workers lie in systems theory. Manor (1989) in exploring the issue of organising accountability for social groupwork, notes the often complex systems involved. The use of systems theory in understanding interaction whether in families or in groups has become increasingly popular. As Iveson (1990, p.9) suggests:

> ...in [systems theory's] simplest form it states that all people and things are parts of systems, each one influencing and being influenced by the others. The usual rules of cause and effect are replaced by interrelatedness and circularity.

The emphasis on understanding and intervening in the process rather than addressing the content of what family members are saying requires similar skills on the part of the family worker to those required of group workers. Social workers often work with families which are involved with many systems (e.g. workplace, school, extended family) where interactions between family members have become stuck in repetitive patterns. These patterns of interaction, although sometimes damaging, particularly to the family member seen as 'the problem', nevertheless keep the family members involved with each other. The worker uses knowledge and skills in order to help the family members find other more positive ways of relating. There has been an increase in recent years of models of systems work with families, or family therapy, based on a greater sharing of information and power between the worker and family members. This way of working is exemplified in the work of De Shazer (1985, 1988); O'Hanlon and Weiner-Davis (1989) and in the work of the London based Brief Therapy Centre, for example Lethem (1994).

Social workers involved in working with complex systems whether in the context of families or groups need to be aware of the interlocking influences of those systems. They also need to have an ability to become involved in the interaction of the system with which they are working as

Fig. 1
Interlocking systems which influenced the collection of the data

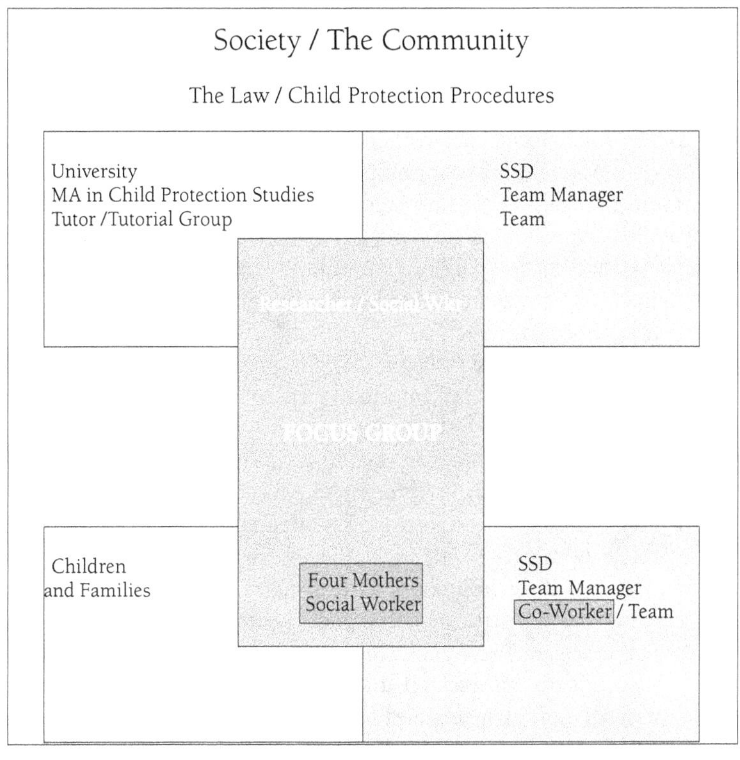

well as the ability to stand back and take a broader view in order to keep a focus on the aims of the work.

As will be explored further in relation to managing focus groups as a method of collecting research data, the researcher needs to know how and when to intervene in the group interaction in order to facilitate the generation of data, at the same time as being alert to the effect on research participants not least because of their responsibilities outside the group. This is particularly relevant when carrying out research concerning sensitive topics. Fig. 1 highlights the interlocking systems involved in the data collection in the study referred to in this paper.

Observational and communication skills as well as a sense of timing of appropriate interventions is an essential part of social work with families, with 'treatment' groups and with research groups. Douglas (1978) and Butler and Wintram (1991) discuss the limitations of discussion/verbal techniques when working with groups. Butler and Wintram (1991, p.56) explain how:

> A woman may have had specific educational abilities which have been ignored or undermined, which have left her feeling inferior to others even before she hears them speak or tries to make contributions herself.

It is necessary for social workers to develop skills and techniques to enable them to both communicate themselves and to facilitate communication between adults and children both in families and in groups. This is essential in carrying out informed assessments as well as in carrying out 'change work' with families and groups. An example of these skills is often evident in the chairing by social workers of complex multi agency meetings such as 'core groups' within child protection procedures where different professional value positions as well as ongoing assessment and evaluation of information play a part in the process of decision making.

An ability to both communicate oneself and to facilitate communication between research participants in order to collect information about the topic which interests the researcher is essential for group based research. Butler and Wintram (1991) highlight the diversity in backgrounds and communication skills of group work participants. This diversity is echoed in the case of my research participants although they too share some significant common experiences. These experiences were central to the research data and very valuable to the research study. An ability to both communicate with research group members and to facilitate communication between them in order to provide important research data is an essential skill for researchers. Social work practitioners should have this skill.

This discussion has explored some of the knowledge and skills which social workers have and which they can apply when carrying out practitioner research. Skills in observation, timing and communication have been highlighted as have a knowledge of systems and ways of intervening in them whilst remaining alert to the aims of the overall purpose of the worker's involvement with participants, whether a family or a stranger group. This section of the paper has also addressed the ways in which contemporary practitioner skills are underpinned by a value base of anti oppression and empowerment and the ways in which this impacts on the carrying out of those skills.

These values, knowledge and skills will now be explored further within the context of carrying out a small scale qualitative study and in particular the use of focus groups as a means of collecting the research data.

The research: a small scale study involving mothers of children who had been sexually abused

The study involved a literature review and the collection of fieldwork data from four mothers, all of whom had experienced statutory child protection procedures because their children (one daughter in each family) had been sexually abused. The research aimed to discover better ways of supporting women in these circumstances based on their own views of the investigative process and their needs post investigation.

The key findings of the research were:

1. Mothers lose their role as 'good mothers' in Western societies when their children have been sexually abused, They are blamed, and blame themselves for the abuse. Like their children, they are also victims of the perpetrator's grooming.
2. The loss of role fundamentally affects the mothers' sense of personal identity and status within the wider family and community.
3. The local authority is more likely to take care proceedings when the mother believes the perpetrator rather than the child.
4. Groupwork with other mothers with similar experiences is effective in helping each other to build a new role.

A focus group: the methodology chosen

The four mothers had worked together in a treatment group set up by a local social services department during a three month period prior to the study. At the conclusion of the groupwork programme the mothers had decided to continue to meet in order to raise public and professional awareness of the needs of mothers whilst supporting each other and other mothers who had experienced the trauma of their children being sexually abused

I had encountered some difficulty in locating a research sample in my employing authority and approached this group of mothers for their help in collecting information for my research. The four mothers readily agreed to become my research participants and in return I agreed to work with them following the study's data collection to help them to raise public and professional awareness and to provide support for other mothers. I had already decided to use a method of data collection involving group interviewing and the reasons for this are highlighted below.

Focus groups provide a technique as a means of collecting 'fieldwork data' in research within the broad category of group interviewing. They offer a way of gathering a lot of information in a short period of time. Importantly, the group process generates information about the topic in that the group members' interaction generates both questions and answers. This is useful particularly when a literature search has revealed little about the topic in which the researcher is interested. This particular technique has developed mainly from market research although Robert Merton, a social scientist, used this method to explore the persuasiveness of wartime propaganda efforts (Merton and Kendall, 1946).

The group process in focus groups is essential in relation to the gathering of data. As Morgan (1988, p.12) states:

> The hallmark of focus groups is the explicit use of the group interaction to produce data and insights that would be less accessible without the interaction found in a group.

To assist with the data collection, the researcher or 'moderator' (Morgan, 1988) prepares beforehand 'topics' or areas of interest. These arise out of questions to which the researcher hopes to find answers. It is important to remember that these 'areas of interest' are only initial guides or 'hooks' on which to hang the information which is produced. As the information is generated, the researcher must remain alert and be prepared to modify and discard her/his initial hypotheses.

Walker (1985, p.78) explains the role of the group interviewer/ researcher or 'moderator' as being to:

> ...conduct a 'steered conversation' rather than an interview. Respondents must be left as free as possible to express themselves, and the moderator's job is mainly to nudge the conversation progressively into the more fruitful channels.

Social work skills already addressed in relation to communication are invaluable in achieving this task. The group members in my study came from different backgrounds and had different experiences although they had shared the important common experience of their children being sexually abused. Facilitating the discussion in order that each group member was able to contribute as fully as possible to the group discussion was a crucial task in my role as researcher. This contributed to the richness of the data collected.

The task of 'nudging' the conversation as described above using this research methodology should nevertheless leave control with the research participants. This is important given the value base of social work practitioners/researchers which adheres to anti oppressive practice. As Morgan (1988, p.18) states:

> The key point is that focus groups offer a stronger mechanism for placing control over...interaction in the hands of the participants rather than the researcher.

Apart from the opportunities for mutual support which this methodology offers, it affords more protection to the research participants because they participate in the giving of information as a group rather than as individuals. Butler and Wintram (1991, p.8) in discussing the lives of the women they worked with as local authority social workers highlight both the women's exploitation and their 'fear, isolation and loneliness...These three factors intertwined, forming their own perfect prism'. Interviewing individually women who have experienced this 'perfect prism' as a practitioner researcher to learn about their experiences might place them at a disadvantage because of the power imbalance in the relationship, however carefully the researcher explains her role. The collective strength, which the members of a research group have, acts as some protection for them in relation to feeling they do not have to co-operate with the provision of data for the research if to do so causes them too much distress.

Initially I had explored the possibility of organising a 'stranger group' i.e. mothers who had no previous contact. However when this aim could not be fulfilled I was fortunate to find an already existing group of 'non abusing' mothers in a different county as already explained. Their major motivation for participating in the research was to help others to avoid the suffering they had experienced; this has been stated by other research participants involved in studies relating to sensitive topics (Roberts and Taylor, 1993; Dempster, 1993). This aim of participants places on the researcher an ethical responsibility not only to disseminate the findings of the research but to try to ensure that they are used to inform services which are set up to help people who are involved in them - in the case of the study referred to in this paper, families and professionals involved in statutory child protection procedures.

A major factor in planning my study was that it should adhere to anti-oppressive practice and to feminist ideals of empowerment of women and sensitivity to their needs. The participants were mothers who had undergone a major crisis in their lives - 'the powerless [rather] than the powerful' (Roberts, 1992, p.180) and had experienced intrusion into their lives by statutory agencies. These issues plus the sensitive and emotionally powerful nature of the topic were central in the design of the study. Importantly I had to ensure that my need to obtain information from mothers who had experienced 'the emotional earthquake' (Salter, 1988, p.56) of discovering that someone they loved had sexually abused their child would cause them minimum further distress. I was also aware that throughout the research process, the participants would be, probably, the main carers and therefore responsible for the ongoing nurturing and protection of vulnerable children. As noted earlier (Figure 1), research participants are members of interlocking systems which could not be ignored.

My prepared topics for the focus group meetings related first to the emotional impact on mothers of the shock of discovering that a loved and trusted family member had sexually abused their children and second their experiences of the statutory child protection procedures in the aftermath of this discovery. The effect of returning again to the very painful memories of their experiences within the context of the focus group discussions was extremely distressing for the mothers, although they had worked together for three months in the 'non abusing parents' group set up by the social services department and had stated that as a result of this group work they already felt much stronger. Nevertheless, despite their distress, they decided that they wanted to continue with the focus groupwork and supported each other in doing so. They said at the completion of the focus group that the process had helped them to discover further insights for themselves which they felt were important in their continuing efforts to become emotionally stronger.

An important person in this research was one of the group's leaders, a local authority social worker, who, it was agreed, would participate in the focus group meetings and could, thus, support the participants afterwards. This was essential since I had to return to my own job as a local authority social worker, in another county, immediately following the meetings. Focus group meetings were arranged during the school day when the mothers were available to participate because they were free from their carer responsibilities.

The effect on the group participants of providing the information for the study reinforced for me the necessity of planning very carefully the support system for group members particularly when the topic is so sensitive and painful. This support is important primarily for the participants but also for the researcher: my experience led me to believe that I could not have continued with the collection of the information had I not been able to trust the mutual support and strength of the group members, including the group worker.

Having been present throughout the focus group meetings the participants' groupworker was also helpful in relation to a particular challenge for me as a social worker in that it helped me to remain in the researcher role which requires objectivity and attention to the task of collecting research data. This is particularly difficult when one's professional role as a practitioner holds different responsibilities involving emotional support and help with problem solving. The two roles can become confused and unrealistic expectations can be raised. Having a co-worker who can help with these needs was extremely helpful.

Support for the participants was set up by themselves, their group leader and myself in meetings before the focus group meetings began. Similarly discussions took place concerning tape recordings of the group discussions for the purposes of analysis and what should happen to the tapes i.e. who owned them. It was agreed that summaries of the information from each meeting should be given to participants at the beginning of the next meeting by myself and that typed summaries of all the meetings should be sent to the participants before the final meeting in order that they could correct them before they were incorporated into my report/dissertation. It was also agreed that the participants should receive their own copies of the dissertation. This jointly negotiated contract, which gave equal power to the research participants, owed much to my social work training and skills in working in partnership with families and groups.

An important agreement in empowering the research participants further was that we should meet with my managers together to inform them of the research findings and of our ideas for incorporating better into the child protection procedures the needs of mothers. This meeting has led to a pilot study in one local authority to explore these suggested changes further.

Conclusion

This paper has explored some of the knowledge and skills which are central to social workers' professional tasks in the field of child and family work within a framework of working in partnership with service users. It has suggested that a knowledge of systems theory and skills based on it in relation to bringing about changes for family and group members is important. Central to these skills are those relating to observation and to communication between themselves and between members of families and groups. The paper has returned throughout to the importance of informing and empowering service users and sees this as a necessary value base to all professional social work.

The participants in this research have stated that their involvement in the focus group meetings and the information they have acquired as a result has played a major part in empowering them. Since the study was concluded, they have given presentations at several conferences and teaching venues in universities and in social services departments as a means of furthering their aims to raise public and professional awareness of the needs of mothers of children who have been sexually abused. They have also written a booklet along with a team of social workers, designed to help mothers, which they produce and sell at their presentations in order to raise funds. These funds will enable the group to hold a national conference of mothers' groups in the near future.

The research participants have also completed a bid for a National Lottery grant to fund setting up eventually a national network of support for mothers. In order to authenticate the need for a national support network for mothers, as required by the National Lottery Board, sections of the completed application form contain material taken by the mothers directly from the research dissertation. Through their involvement in a piece of practitioner research, the four mothers' original aims have been realised in a way which has empowered them and ensured that they have remained in control of the process.

Note

The good news was recently received that the Lottery Board did award the full amount for which the mothers applied.

References

Brannen, J. and O'Brien, M. (eds.) (1996) *Children in Families: Research and Policy.* Basingstoke: Falmer Press.

Brown, A. (1994) *Groupwork.* Aldershot: Ashgate Publishing Co.

Butler, S. and Wintram, C. (1991) *Feminist Groupwork* . London: Sage.

CCETSW (1994) *Child Care: Competences for the Post Qualifying and Advanced Awards, Professional Development in the Personal Social Services Working Paper 1.* London: CCETSW.

Dempster, H.L. (1993) 'The aftermath of child sexual abuse: women's perspectives' in Waterhouse, L. (ed.) *Child Abuse and Child Abusers - Protection and Prevention*. London: Jessica Kingsley.

De Shazer, S. (1985) *Keys to Solution in Brief Therapy*. New York: Norton.

De Shazer, S. (1988) *Clues: Investigating Solution in Brief Therapy*. New York: Norton.

Douglas, T. (1978) *Basic Groupwork*. London: Tavistock Publications.

DOH (1989) *An Introduction to the Children Act*. London: HMSO.

DOH (1995) *Child Protection - Messages from Research*. London: HMSO.

Fuller, R. and Petch, A. (1995) *Practitioner Research: The Reflexive Social Worker*. Buckingham: Open University Press.

Heap, K. (1988) 'The worker and the group process: a dilemma revisited', *Groupwork*, 1, pp.17-29.

Iveson, C. (1990) *Whose Life? Community Care of Older People and their Families*. London: Brief Therapy Press.

Letham, J. (1994) *Moved to Tears, Moved to Action - Solution Focused Brief Therapy with Women and Children*. London: Brief Therapy Press.

Manor, O. (1989) 'Organising accountability for social groupwork: more choices', *Groupwork*, 2, 108-122.

Merton, R.K. and Kendall, P.L. (1946) 'The focused interview', *The American Journal of Sociology*, 51, pp.541-557.

Morgan, D.L. (1988) *Focus Groups as Qualitative Research*. London: Sage Publications.

Mullender, A. and Ward, D. (1991) *Self-Directed Groupwork - Users Take Action for Empowerment*. London: Whiting and Birch.

O'Hanlon W.H. and Weiner-Davis, M. (1989) *In Search of Solutions*. New York: Norton.

Roberts, H. (1992) *Women's Health Matters*. London: Routledge.

Roberts, J. and Taylor, C. (1993) 'Sexually abused children and young people speak out' in Waterhouse, L. (ed.) *Child Abuse and Child Abusers - Protection and Prevention*. London: Jessica Kingsley.

Salter, A.C. (1988) *Treating Child Sex Offenders and Victims - A Practical Guide*. London: Sage.

Walker, R.L. (1985) Applied Qualitative Research. Aldershot: Gower.

This chapter first published in 1996 in *Groupwork* Vol. 9(2), pp.139-153

At the time of writing, the author was a Part-Time Lecturer in Post-Qualifying Studies (Child Care)

Enhancing research usefulness with adapted focus groups

Alice M. Home

Abstract: *Focus groups are a data collection method in which people reflect together on selected themes or questions. This method is a good way for practitioners to begin doing research, as it makes use of skills familiar to groupworkers. This paper first describes the goals and characteristics of these groups, showing how to plan and facilitate them as well as how to analyse the data they produce. The article then illustrates how adapted focus groups were used to complement and follow up on a survey of multiple role women students. The classic format was adapted, to take the research context into account and to achieve dual goals of data collection and dissemination. Using focus groups increased the cost of the survey but resulted in more grounded, practical and accessible findings. Groupworkers are invited to experiment with this research method and report on their experiences.*

keywords: *focus groups; women students; nominal group; delphi technique*

Groupworkers may hesitate to research their practice, either due to concerns about how results will be used or because they lack relevant skills and instruments (Galinsky and Schopler, 1993). Similarly, many researchers are reluctant to use group-based data collection techniques because they are unsure how to manage possible bias. This concern has led to the development of research methods designed to control or monitor group influence, while gleaning the benefits only a group can bring. One such method is the focus group interview, which brings people together to reflect on a limited number of questions or themes in the context of others' views (Patton, 1990). This paper describes focus groups, then illustrates how they were used in one research project to deepen understanding of the findings and to enhance their usefulness.

Focus groups are a good way for practitioners to begin doing research, as they make use of planning and facilitating skills that are already part of workers' practice repertoire. This lessens the insecurity which often plagues skilled practitioners as they contemplate incorporating research into their work. These workers know that groups have the potential to generate creative thinking and solutions which reflect members' diverse experiences.

However, the very qualities which make groups attractive to

practitioners can also limit their usefulness as research tools. Group influence can shape members' behaviour thereby producing good individual and collective outcomes, while interaction allows spontaneous sharing of experiences and ideas. Yet, both influence and interaction can result in some members' contributions being heard and valued more than others', so that the final outcome may not fully reflect the group experience. For researchers, this means group-based data collection can produce biased results.

In an attempt to manage bias, researchers have developed two techniques which strictly control group interaction and influence. Both seek to tap the opinion of groups of people with expertise in a given area, with a view to identifying zones of convergence and divergence. Members of a Delphi 'group' remain anonymous and do not meet. Rather, they provide individual written responses to several open questions, then clarify, revise and react to repeat summaries of their grouped ideas until either consensus or stability is achieved. The Nominal group is a group in name only (Lauffer, 1982), because member interaction and influence are tightly controlled during meetings. Members of these heterogeneous groups write individual responses to specific questions. Each response is recorded and posted for all to see and each point is clarified to ensure shared understanding by all participants. Usually, there is no interaction prior to the final priority-setting vote, but some groups allow members to discuss results of a preliminary vote before making a final decision (Mayer and Ouellet, 1991).

Both techniques ensure all participants have an equal opportunity to have their ideas heard, such that the final result takes the full range of member opinion into account. This means these techniques are useful in certain situations. The Delphi technique allows a meeting of minds among geographically isolated experts, who cannot easily interact face-to-face. For example, this method was used to tap the opinions of experts across Canada on the subject of social work education for First Nations peoples. The Nominal technique can be helpful where a rapid solution is needed for a complex problem. In an existing group, this technique can be used to control conflicts, power struggles or status differences which might hamper effective problem-solving.

However, the strict control of group process also limits its capacity to enhance research. Just as many workers bemoan the inattention to group process in structured education models (Papell and Rothman, 1980), practitioner-researchers want to take full advantage of the group's potential. For '...groups are not just a convenient way to accumulate the individual knowledge of their members. They give rise synergistically to insights and solutions that would not come about without them' (Brown, Collins and Duguid, 1989, p.40). The focus group method differs from the Nominal and Delphi techniques by its emphasis on harnessing rather than controlling group process.

Focus groups: goals and characteristics

This group interview method, developed originally as a marketing tool, has gained popularity in the social sciences in the last decade. Focus groups are more efficient than individual interviews, in that data can be collected from more people in less time and sometimes at lower cost (Patton, 1990). The usual procedure is to form several small, homogeneous groups, which meet once for one to two hours to discuss a topic of interest to the researcher. The main goal is to learn about the experiences and perspectives of people who have either work or life experience in a given area (Morgan, 1988).

Focus groups can stand alone as a primary data collection method or they can be used in conjunction with other approaches. When used as a self-contained research method, the results should be triangulated or compared with other sources or types of data (Denzin, 1978). For example, dissimilar groups (such as men and women) can reflect on the same topic or some individual interviews can be carried out to supplement focus group data. In one action-research project, workers were brought together to reflect on the usefulness of a respite care service for families experiencing stress. Each worker was also asked to complete a brief questionnaire. Comparison of the two data sources allowed researchers to validate information, while showing that focus groups produce data not available through individual questionnaires. The group data revealed that just knowing respite care was available made some mothers feel more secure about their ability to cope with unexpected crises. The researchers also discovered that this informal service helped mothers who had never before used child care overcome the fear and guilt which had made them hesitate (Home and Darveau-Fournier, 1995).

In many research projects, however, focus groups serve both as supplementary data and as a way of compensating for weaknesses in the primary research method. Focus groups can be planned early in the research process to develop interview or survey questions or they can follow up on participant observation, interviews or a survey (Morgan, 1988). The latter use allows researchers to gain new perspectives on the meaning and implications of the findings.

Planning focus groups

Groupworkers know that successful intervention requires careful planning and solid facilitating skills. Similarly, the time invested in systematic planning pays off in higher quality, more relevant focus group data. Several planning issues familiar to groupworkers need to be addressed: ethics, costs, number and size of groups, recruitment, level of structure and facilitator involvement (Morgan, 1988). A preliminary question, however, is whether focus groups are an appropriate method in a given research situation. Practitioners know they should select the groupwork method only when they are satisfied that it is the best way to meet client need (Home, 1985). Focus groups should not be used just to save time or money, nor should they be selected if interviews or participant observation would be more effective in achieving research goals. They are most useful when participants are knowledgeable about and interested in the topic. The participants may not feel comfortable discussing sensitive or controversial subjects in a group of strangers.

Once the practitioner-researcher is sure focus groups are suitable, initial planning decisions can be made, taking into account ethical and time/cost factors. Participants are asked to respect confidentiality and access to raw data is restricted. The practitioner-researcher specifies the purposes for which data will be used, while assuring participants that their anonymity will be protected in any reports (Patton, 1990). Time and cost considerations are similar to some found in groupwork practice. As the group meetings last only a few hours, there is a danger of underestimating the time needed for such tasks as recruiting participants, organising meeting rooms and training facilitators. Costs can be contained more easily if the researcher acts as facilitator, but a realistic budget must allow for room and equipment rental, travel, payment of recorders (and perhaps participants) and transcription of tapes.

Research goals are the main determinant of number and size of groups but budget and time constraints may also play a role. Exploratory research requires fewer groups than projects seeking specific knowledge about different subpopulations. One rule of thumb is to plan an initial number of three to eight groups, adjusting the final number to ensure enough data are available to answer research questions. Groups usually include six to twelve participants. Smaller groups are indicated when individual reactions are sought to specific questions. Larger groups can be harder to manage, but they are more productive and cost-effective in early, exploratory research. Over recruiting by 20 per cent to cover for 'no shows' is a good idea, regardless of planned group size (Morgan, 1988).

Recruitment is a key planning issue, as all population subgroups relevant to the research goals should be represented. Once these are identified, practitioner-researchers should devise suitable strategies, which can include telephone screening, use of personal networks and a few informant interviews with target subgroup members. As in groupwork practice, decisions must be made about balancing homogeneity and heterogeneity of members' backgrounds on such factors as age, gender, race and class. While willingness to share experiences depends more on perceived similarity than on actual commonalities (Morgan, 1988), homogeneous groups run less risk of encountering severe conflict or refusal to speak up (Patton, 1990).

Group structure and facilitator involvement

The final planning decision involves level of structure and facilitator involvement. Typically, focus groups are structured around a few specific questions or topics, which are discussed with the active help of a facilitator (Patton, 1990). This choice ensures desired topics are covered, while allowing easier management of overly dominant or reticent individuals, discussion getting off track or 'group think' stifling minority opinion (Patton, 1990; Morgan, 1988). Lower facilitator involvement can be useful, however, in exploratory research which seeks to have participants identify issues of high interest and importance. Within any one group, participants can be asked both to identify issues and to discuss specific questions. Another option is to plan a combined design, such that self-managed groups first identify key issues to be discussed later by more structured groups (Morgan, 1988).

Facilitating a focus group effectively requires considerable skill (Patton, 1990). General principles are to suggest group norms around listening and equal participation, while emphasising that the facilitator is there to learn from the participants. Most groups begin with an autobiographical statement by each member, which serves as an icebreaker while deterring 'groupthink' (Janis, 1982). This is usually followed by discussion of questions in a sequenced order. The group ends with individual summary statements and/or a summary by the facilitator.

Observations are captured mainly by audiotaping, to minimise intrusiveness and confidentiality problems which can accompany videotaping. A second researcher usually looks after taping and takes field notes, to ensure data are both usable and complete. The recorder's observations can be analysed along with transcribed verbal interactions.

Data can be analysed using either the ethnographic summary or content analysis method. The former identifies initial and emerging topics which serve to organise a large number of direct quotes. Content analysis identifies themes from a few initial transcripts, which are used to code and categorise data. Frequency of mention can then be calculated and themes illustrated by selected quotes. In both methods, independent examination of transcripts by two or more researchers enhances the validity of the findings (Patton, 1990).

Final report style reflects choices made about analysis. The ethnographic approach blends discussion summaries with many direct quotes, while content analysis combines summary tables and descriptive summaries with a few illustrative quotes (Morgan, 1988). Regardless of style, it is essential that the method and analysis be described systemically, to ensure this qualitative research is seen as credible. Furthermore, the report should be presented in a clear style, including just enough detail to ensure understanding and create interest. The target audience is likely to read a concise, clear, attractively presented report, even if little time is available.

Adapted focus groups as a complementary data source: an example

Focus groups were used by the author to follow up on a survey of women who carry family and job responsibilities while studying social work, nursing or adult education. This subject was chosen because increasing numbers of social work students are either employed or carry family responsibilities and many combine all three roles (Lennon, 1991). This study followed up on earlier exploratory work, which found that students with three roles experience intense role demands and chronic role strain but receive mainly informal rather than institutional support (Home, 1993). Survey goals were to examine the relationship between role demands (expectations from each role), role strain (overload, conflict and contagion), stress and support. The researcher wanted to find out if any specific groups of multiple role women were at higher risk for stress or strain and to identify institutional supports that might reduce vulnerability. Nearly 500 students in 17 Canadian university programmes participated in the survey. In many respects, this survey shared the advantages of disadvantages of other quantitative-descriptive studies focused on examining relationships between variables (Tripodi, Fellin and Meyer, 1985).

This study was supported by a strategic grant[1], which stipulated that results should be made available to a wide audience of potential users and policy makers, with a view to promoting change. The researcher was aware that survey findings are shared primarily with a limited number of academics and researchers, usually only at the end of the project. Consequently, the potential impact on policy and practice is limited. In addition, surveys have an inherent weakness of dealing with issues in a superficial manner. Even though most of the research instruments were developed directly from the author's qualitative data, there was a risk of not fully understanding what the findings meant. It would be difficult, therefore, to trace implications for practice, education and policy. Identifying strategies for promoting change would be even harder.

The researcher decided to use focus groups to reach out to a wide audience of potential users, who would reflect on the meaning and implications of initial findings as well as suggest action. Planning decisions were guided by the context coupled with the dual research goals of data collection and dissemination. A national, bilingual context made it essential to tap regional diversity, so feedback sessions were planned for western, eastern and central Canada as well as for Quebec. Key subpopulations included representatives of diverse interest groups (unions, employers, workers, students) from a variety of health care, educational and social service settings. Both the research design and recruitment strategy had to be uniform enough to permit comparison yet sufficiently flexible to accommodate regional differences. Two focus groups were planned for each region except for central Canada, where a third group was needed for linguistic reasons.

The particular context and goals of this research also led to adaptations in the classic format. While focus groups are usually homogeneous, these groups assembled representatives of different professions and interest groups. Members were united by a primary concern for either educational or workplace implications, which served as the criterion for choice of group. Another adaptation was to introduce the hour-long groups with a research presentation and to close the sessions with a plenary, which brought the different groups together to review main points and decide on action. The opening presentation was designed to share key findings and prepare participants to discuss them. It was also a recruitment strategy, designed to attract people who might be able to influence policy or practice. A refreshment break to promote regional networking was also part of the plan.

Several recruitment strategies were devised to ensure that about a hundred representatives of the various targeted subpopulations would attend. The two national partner associations publicised the feedback sessions in their newsletters, which were distributed to schools of social work or nursing and to many individual faculty members. The sessions were publicised in an adult education newsletter as well. Some financial assistance was offered to allow the seventeen sampled schools to send a representative. Using partners, personal networks and a locally-hired resource person, a list of 235 names was compiled for the four sites. Wherever possible, the letter of invitation and short descriptive pamphlet were sent to a specific person rather than to the organisation. This carefully designed recruitment strategy succeeded in attracting over a hundred participants, who reflected the desired mix of professions and settings.

Experienced group facilitators led each group, using written guidelines which were explained in a brief training session. A recorder took notes, as it was felt audiotaping might complicate ethics procedures and inhibit some participants from speaking freely. The groups warmed up with each member highlighting which results were most relevant for his/her educational institution or workplace, then the groups considered three questions. They identified policies or practices which supported multiple role women in their setting, they noted obstacles to establishing effective supportive measures and recommended strategies for regional and national action. The questions and general format of the first session were evaluated by each participant, using a one-page questionnaire. The results were considered along with observations of the research team, leading to minor modifications which improved subsequent sessions.

As in most qualitative research, analysis began as soon as the first focus group data were available (Miles and Huberman, 1984). The researcher selected thematic content analysis over the ethnographic summary method, because of the specific nature of the research questions (Morgan, 1988). A second, more practical reason for this choice was that few direct quotes were available due to the decision to take notes rather than use audiotapes. As the group discussions were highly structured, the researcher chose Miles and Huberman's (1984) systematic technique for coding, displaying and describing data. This procedure mixes deductive and inductive methods. An initial coding scheme, developed from the question themes and research goals, was refined after two members of the research team read the recorders' summaries of the first groups. Data from the remaining groups were classified using the initial codes, supplemented by others derived inductively from later groups. Data from each group were coded by one research assistant and revised by another in order to enhance validity (Patton, 1990). Subsequent analysis involved noting frequency of mention and illustrative examples of subthemes, followed by preparation of descriptive data display tables. The three main themes reflected the focus group questions. Theme areas included effective existing policies and practices, obstacles hindering supportive measures and suggestions for change. In addition, data were grouped by workplace or educational focus, while further analysis allowed identification of professional and regional similarities and differences.

Finding effective ways to disseminate both survey and qualitative data was an important reason for adding the focus group method. One suggested action strategy was to distribute regional summaries to participants, inviting them to share what they had learned with others in their university, college, association or agency. Accordingly, regional summaries were distributed both to participants and to invited others who had not been able to attend. A second dissemination strategy was to move beyond traditional scholarly publications through the preparation of practical documents, which would be accessible to a wide readership of potential research users. The main survey findings were combined with focus group data to produce two short, readable publications targeting different audiences. A summary pamphlet was designed to reach multiple role women and those who work closely with them (instructors, colleagues and supervisors). A 12-page guide was distributed to a more restricted audience of key people, organisations and institutions, including many libraries. Both documents began by summarising major research goals and findings, ending with focus group data which highlighted practical implications for the relevant target group.

Conclusion: to what extent were focus groups useful?

Using adapted focus groups was a successful strategy for enriching this survey research and for enhancing its practical relevance. First, rich qualitative data were obtained which allowed researchers to understand and explain the survey results more fully. For example, one student who ran between her part-time job, her elderly mother, her children and her studies, said she learned nothing about nursing the first year. But she learned to study in little bits of time, to drive in all kinds of weather, to survive on little money and to work despite lack of sleep. She brought alive the concept of role overload and showed that many women cope despite tremendous obstacles.

A second advantage of using focus groups was that many more people had a chance to hear and reflect on results than would have been the case if the researcher had limited dissemination to traditional academic conferences and articles. Over a hundred feedback session participants heard the findings and several hundred others received the summary pamphlets or handbooks. Thirdly, the focus group data enhanced the chances that these documents would have an impact on their readers. Specific suggestions and change strategies were included in both publications. For example, the pamphlet advised multiple role students to join together for mutual support and social action, while suggesting that instructors and colleagues recognise the heavy load these women bear and work toward making existing policies and practices more flexible. The focus group data on obstacles made the researchers aware of employers' concerns about cost containment. The handbook emphasised partnership and cooperative strategies rather than those requiring major financial investments. Similarly, focus group participants said that striving to increase support for multiple role women should be presented in a positive fashion. The handbook stated that 'combining employment, family and education is a growing trend' and that 'finding creative ways to adapt' to this new reality would help individuals and their institutions prepare for the 21st century (Home, Hinds, Malenfant and Boisjoli, 1995, p.10). As a result of this strategy, the documents were so well received that the researcher was deluged with requests for additional copies.

The only disadvantage to using focus groups in this study was the high cost. Organising and analysing the focus groups monopolised the research associate's time for six months, greatly adding to the cost of the study. However, given the overall cost of conducting a survey, the payoff in more grounded, practical and accessible findings was worth the time, money and effort expended.

This paper has described and illustrated one approach to using groups to enhance research. Focus groups are not easy to plan and facilitate, but they hold promise as a practical way of reducing the gap between research and practice. It is hoped that groupwork practitioners and researchers will experiment with some of the ideas in this article and report on their experiences.

Note

1. This study was supported by a grant from the Strategic Grants Division, Social Sciences and Humanities Research Council of Canada. Cora Hinds (School of Nursing, University of Ottawa) was co-investigator, while the Canadian Association of Schools of Social Work and the Canadian Association of University Schools of Nursing were partners in this research.

References

Brown, J., Collins, A. and Duguid, P. (1989) 'Situated cognition and the culture of learning', *Educational Researcher,* 18(1), pp.32-42.

Denzin, N. (1978) *The Research Act*. Second Edition. New York: McGraw-Hill.

Galinsky, M. and Schopler, J. (1993) 'Social group work competence: our strengths and challenges' in Kurland, R. and Salmon, R. (eds.) *Group Work Practice in a Troubled Society*. New York: Haworth, pp.33-44.

Home, A. and Darveau-Fournier, L. (1995) 'Respite child care: A support and empowerment strategy for families in a high-risk community', *Prevention in Human Services*, 12(1), pp.69-82.

Home, A. (1993) 'The juggling act: The multiple role woman in social work education', *Canadian Social Work Review,* 10(2), pp.157-182.

Home, A. (1985) 'Intervention with groups' in Yelaja, S. (ed.) *An Introduction to Social Work Practice in Canada*. Scarborough, Ont.: Prentice-Hall, pp. 69-89.

Home, A., Hinds, C., Malenfant, B. et Boisjoli, D. (1995) *Managing a Job, a Family and Studies: A Guide for Educational Institutions and the Workplace*. Ottawa: University of Ottawa. This document can be obtained from ERIC Clearinghouse on Adult, Career and Vocational Education.

Janis, I. (1982) *Groupthink*. Second Edition. Boston: Houghton-Mifflin.

Lauffer, A. (1982) *Assessment Tools*. Beverly Hills: Sage.

Lennon, T. (1991) *Statistics on Social Work Education in the United States: 1991*. Alexandria, Virginia: CSWE.

Mayer, R. and Ouellet, F. (1990) *Méthodologie de Recherche pour les Intervenants Sociaux*. Boucherville: Gaëtan Morin.

Miles, M. et Huberman, M. (1984) Qualitative Data Analysis. Beverly Hills: Sage.

Morgan, D. (1988) 'Focus groups as qualitative research', *Qualitative Research Methods*. Volume 16. Newbury Park: Sage.

Papell, C. and Rothman, B. (1983) 'Relating the mainstream model of social work with groups to group psychotherapy and the structured group approach', *Social Work with Groups*, 3, pp.5-22.

Patton, M. (1990) *Qualitative Evaluation and Research Methods*. Second Edition. Newbury Park: Sage.

Tripodi, T., Fellin, T. and Meyer, H. (1985) *The Assessment of Social Research*. Itasca: Peacock.

This chapter first published in 1996 in *Groupwork* Vol. 9(2), pp.128-138

At the time of writing, the author was a Professor of Social Work, Dept of Social Work, University of Ottawa

Empowering research process: Using groups in research to empower the people

Asnarulkhadi Abu-Samah

Abstract: *This article discusses how a qualitative research approach is appropriate for research in a context where groups are a central focus. The approach, which is ideologically and philosophically based on the 'second tradition' that values people's interpretation of their social world uses an interactive technique of data collection involving in-depth interviews, follow-up interviews and group discussions. These techniques, administered in a dialogue fashion, generated information which showed that people are becoming empowered through experiencing the participation process within groups in their community. In addition, while sharing and feeding back information within the techniques used, people are learning and becoming empowered. As they became accustomed to this, they began to realise the significance of the research approach used.*

keywords: *interpretative tradition; grounded experiences; empowerment; group discussion*

Introduction: philosophy and ideology in social research

Obtaining and gaining data or information from the people studied is the basic aim of social research. To achieve this, social scientists/researchers such as sociologists, anthropologists, community workers/developers or social workers use different methods of data collection to approach and to understand the subject matter studied. These can be classified broadly into two approaches, quantitative and qualitative. There are philosophical debates and competing views between these two approaches (Bryman, 1988) as to how the researcher should 'treat' social reality: the people to be studied who live in their own world. Social scientists who uphold the positivist viewpoint use approaches such as surveys or questionnaires as their data collection tools to capture and understand the subject matter under scrutiny. This 'positive' tradition believes that social realities and phenomena can be explained 'scientifically', based on the regularities from the data obtained. Most researchers who take this standpoint aim 'not to disturb the world they are studying: their aim, instead, is to trawl their data collecting net quietly through the social world' (Graham and Jones, 1992, p.239).

In contrast to the 'positive' tradition is the interpretive tradition in which an understanding of the social world and the subject matter studied is generated from the people. This second tradition is more concerned with understanding social reality and phenomena, and interprets them from the viewpoint of the people themselves (Denzin, 1970a, 1970b). These are basic principles held by phenomenologists and interactionists. The argument is that human beings are active participants who live in a changing environment. As they interact with the social world in their everyday lives they adapt and adjust to the situation. Thus, the people's active response to social reality possesses some meaning which cannot be interpreted by a snapshot survey. It is through the process of 'going native' with the people that the meaning behind their reactions and actions towards certain situations can be explained.

Working along the same principle, participationists move a step further. Researchers not only aim to understand what meaning and significance the social world has for the people, but also explore the social world, its 'properties' and nature. These are developed, generated and verified by and with the people themselves based on their 'grounded experiences' (Glaser and Strauss, 1967). Concurrently involving the respondents in the whole research process enables them to become active participants in defining and interpreting their actions, collectively and actively with the researcher, which can enhance their understanding about their own living environment. Thus, the notion of empowerment is embedded in this research approach. Further, by taking and shifting the paradigm of researching social realities from 'researcher-centred', where the research problems are predefined or 'controlled' by the researcher, to 'researched-centred', where research issues are being defined and scrutinised together with the people through dialogue, this enhances the values of consciousness raising and empowerment.

Based on this second tradition, this article shows how a research process, by involving the respondents from the initial stage, facilitates them in reflecting on and understanding their actions in community life. This writing is based on a case study of a Malay rural planned village settlement in Malaysia. The aim of the study was to understand the people's participation in community development and community work activities - establishing groups and organising community group-based activities. Each group had its own particular interests, ranging from taking care of community welfare, offering communal services, providing community and adult education, safeguarding vulnerable youths from drug problems, and securing and controlling rights of land possession.

Groups as a central part in the research process

First and foremost, in carrying out social research one has to remember that we, the researchers, are dealing with human beings, individually or collectively in their own living environment. One common feature of people's behaviour is that they live and interact within a group. Groups can take various forms and size; the simplest and smallest may be self-help groups or neighbourhood groups, while the biggest and more complex ones may take the form of associations or one community. Regardless of the size and type of groups, individual life within the group is dynamic. The researcher needs to be sensitive to the context and life of the researched within the respective groups in the community. Therefore, in order to grasp a true picture of people's behaviour, action and endeavour, or in the case of this study people's participation in which individual's experience is the fundamental source of information, it is necessary to study them within the dynamic context of the group. This requires a sensitive and interactive methodological approach, which takes into consideration the group element as a central focus.

The qualitative-ethnographic approach

From this researcher's experience the ethnographic participative approach has particular value for research with and about groups. The interactive techniques of data collection, such as personal in-depth interviews and group discussions, provide a sensitive way of collecting data. The unrestricted and open-ended nature of data collection techniques which are based on guidelines consisting of loosely-formed questions, provide freedom for the respondents to express their views and experiences. The researcher who may follow-up with more probing questions, must listen and record carefully. The techniques have an empowering element, in that respondents have the opportunity to reflect on their past experiences of working as a group and of seeking to achieve group goals.

Qualitative-ethnographic research, which is often denoted as 'thick description' (Greetz, 1975) among anthropologists is holistic in nature and the time spent researching the subject matter is relatively long compared to the survey method. It provides opportunities for the researcher to examine other pertinent and emerging issues related to the subject studied throughout the study period, thus enriching the information collected.

Research as empowerment

The basic principle underlying my research is that the respondents were encouraged to be involved actively in the research process. It was through their direct involvement that the subject matter studied could be scrutinised in depth, based on people's first hand experiences. From the point view of basic research, people's experiences are significant in order to understand and explain in what ways and why they react to the environment. Empowering research moves a step further. Facilitated by the qualitative-ethnographic approach, the research method offers an interactive relationship between the researcher and the respondents, not only in terms of acquiring information but also in terms of its use, during and after enquiry sessions.

The interactive and responsive data collection techniques of in-depth interviews and group discussions were carried out in a dialogue style. The unrestricted, open-ended framework of loosely guidelined questions, encouraged the respondents to explore the subject matter collaboratively with the researcher in a 'non-monopolistic' manner (see Fals-Borda, 1991). These interactive techniques enabled the respondents to be directly involved in this research activity. In this interactive and participative process the relationship between researcher and respondents was not just a researcher-object or researcher-researched relationship, but more a researcher-subjects relationship. Treating people as subjects meant that they had the right to speak and to be heard and minimised manipulation.

In contrast to conventional research, where research questions are predetermined or derived from existing bodies of knowledge, in interactive research questions can be developed and refined throughout the research process. Through an induction and deduction process of acquiring the information from respondents individually and collectively, the subject matter can be understood clearly in the context of peoples' own experiences. By enabling them to explore their own world through dialogue, their involvement as active partners throughout the research is enhanced. This framework of investigation also creates a mutual consciousness between researcher and subjects, and, in this way, a more comprehensive understanding of the subject matter. This can subsequently act as a basis for further 'empowering' action by the subjects, having realised that they have the capability to define needs and problems, and to take action on them.

How these underlying principles have been employed to motivate and mobilise research subjects to engage themselves, and subsequently to benefit from their direct involvement in the research process is explored and discussed below.

'The welcoming tone'

Like any other ethnographic study, meeting the people, the study subjects, was crucial. The importance of their involvement in the research was not only in terms of their position as the source of information, but also in their willingness to participate in the research, and their expectations that the research would be productive for them. This positive attitude towards the research activity was observed clearly during the first meeting, before embarking on the actual data collection activity. In this meeting the issue of data collection techniques excited them. Realising that the method to be used in this study would be quite different from previous studies carried out and experienced by them, one of the respondents requested that the findings be shared with him later:

> It's good to have research like this. I think it is quite different from the previous one...and I would like to see the results from your research later... At least if you can spare me a synopsis or summary of the findings. So, I can know about my village, my people, what they want..., on what they disagree with me. Then I can react on it later, if possible. (Mr Wan)

On another occasion before engaging into a group discussion, one of the respondents from the youth club said:

> That day, you, brother (referring to the researcher), wanted to meet all my friends from Embun Hidayah (name of the youth club). Hah! Today I bring them all. At least they can share in our discussion today. Possible isn't it? You can hear and confirm from them what I narrated to you a few months ago... (Mr Sofi)

Using an interactive data collection technique created a situation which encouraged people's involvement in the research activity. Mobilising the people towards this activity was made possible because the stand taken by the researcher was that the people themselves are more knowledgeable about the environment in which they live. This stand was reiterated by the researcher during the first meeting with respondents (group members from each of the community groups) in the village, as illustrated in the examples below:

> ...to learn from you all how you get engaged with the activity...and share some information that I don't have.

> I am eager to know about your experiences of how you became involved with and organised the activity, if you can share these with me...

These answers were given as a response to questions asked such as: 'Why do you want to know about our activities?' and 'What is so special about us here?'. Within this stimulating interaction with the people, facilitated by open-ended and unstructured interviews used in a dialogic fashion, much information about group activities and the members' involvement was gathered in this preliminary discourse. Respecting their position as subjects who possessed the real experience and knowledge about their community life, and demonstrating the researcher's readiness to learn from them, encouraged them to reveal information. It was also noted during this preliminary dialogue that the subjects, regardless of their gender (members from the men's groups or women's groups) were motivated to show and share how they became involved in organising group activities by inviting the researcher to attend their group meetings. This encouraging and stimulating atmosphere shown by the subjects gradually diminished the researcher's own worries and doubts about carrying out research in women's areas and groups, an issue that has been raised and debated by feminist researchers (Oakley, 1981; Ramazanoglu, 1992; Finch, 1993). The positive attitude and willingness to share experiences is evident from the illustration below:

> Is it okay if I bring along my friends to our meeting today? Both are my neighbours. Yesterday I went to their house and simply invited them... Today they're willing to follow me, to hear about our meeting. They are our group members. Sometimes they join me in the activity. You can ask them questions too! (Mrs Fira)

In a similar vein, on another occasion before the group discussion started, one uninvited participant came and asked permission to participate:

> Can I join the meeting, is it okay or not...? I want to know exactly what's going on. Three days ago you invited my friend but not me to the meeting today. I asked her what's going on. I'm not busy body...She said, if I would like to know, just follow her today, it is a discussion about our group activities. Can I join in? (Mrs Aminah)

In other words, it can be argued that it is the empowering framework of research adopted, allowing people to participate in the information gathering, which mobilised them to engage in the research process.

Choosing the sample

As more information was disclosed by the subjects about their group activities and members involvement, more preliminary data were captured, and this enabled me to develop a sampling strategy, in this case a snowball technique. In relation to studying people's participation in community work and community development activities, the issue of sampling is worth considering. Randomly choosing the community members to be included into the sampling frame or sampling list as advocated by the quantitative method may not reveal a true picture of people's participation. This is because by using such technique, the chances of including individuals who may not be involved in community group activities is great, and this certainly could distort understanding of the subject matter.

The close and interactive relationship with group members in the preliminary dialogue sessions helped to minimise and monitor these issues. Through group members' recommendations, names were gathered. These names were then accumulated and validated along the research process when each respondent was asked about other members' involvement and contribution in their group activity through probing questions incorporated into the interviews, together with the researcher's own observations from attending group meetings, some secondary documents obtained, and a recorded video tape lent by a group. Names that were mentioned at least twice by respondents were interviewed. There are two reasons or rationale for employing this interactive strategy. The first reason was, in relation to the phenomenological aspect of this ethnographic approach, that the understanding of the subject matter (in this case people's participation) should be grasped from the point view of the subjects. Therefore, to misjudge the sample could mislead the understanding of how respondents organised themselves to participate in community work activities. This further has some connection with a second reason, in that only individuals who had experienced the participation process could reflect on those experiences. In reflecting, they empowered themselves by realising that they had the capability to act and decide for themselves. More on this issue is discussed below.

In short, methodologically, the approach used created a situation that encouraged the subjects to participate directly in the research process, and simultaneously acted as a useful device to verify the information gathered through a process of deduction and induction incorporated within the interviewing process.

Induction and deduction process

The qualitative-ethnographic approach enables both induction and deduction to take place simultaneously in the research process. It is a cyclic process of verifying data gathered by checking and cross checking both with and between respondents. Starting from the first day of observation and interview, data were gathered and some ideas were conceptualised, deduced and adopted. As the interviews continued more ideas were developed and concepts generated. These, and other interrelated concepts, were clarified and verified by converting them into more questions, a process of analytical induction. All ideas and concepts deduced from the last interview were checked against another respondent in next session. Therefore, it was within and between the interview(s) that deduction and induction took place which verified ideas and concepts as data accumulated. These interrelated ideas and concepts then emerged as themes, which guided and focused the researcher's probing and prompting questions until they reached saturation and refinement.

The checking and cross-checking process in this study not only took place between respondents within a single method but also between methods. Through paying careful attention during the interviews, some important keywords, phases or clues were jotted down as theoretical memos, and personal observations and impressions were also recorded in field notes as part of the deductive procedure. The researcher also engaged in the deductive process by making notes while listening to what the respondents said in the interview tapes. Again, these data were checked against the deductive ideas from memos and personal impressions recorded from earlier notes. In these ways grounded concepts or categories and their relationships were generated. These interrelated concepts were again refined, compared and checked against the themes generated from transcribed interviews. Through deduction and induction (interchangeably at this stage), more concise concepts and themes grounded in the data were constructed. Both the concepts and themes were then brought back to share and debate with the respondents through the follow-up interviews and group discussions.

This process was possible because the qualitative-ethnographic approach allows the researcher to step backwards and forwards during the research process, internalising and testing data against other respondents or sources of evidence, either by questioning or observing, to set the meaning in context. In other words, the concepts developed during data collection are validated throughout the research process by triangulating (Denzin, 1970) within and between the methods, with the same respondent and between respondents, during the in-depth interviews and group discussions. By triangulating within and between different sources of evidence, data collected were enriched and thus able to overcome the limitations of using a single method. The multi-method approach also allowed for convergent lines of interrogation of different sources of evidence, thus, eliminating bias and promoting the validity of the data collected.

Reflecting and sharing information

The in-depth interview and group discussion were the techniques used to gather information from the respondents. Intensive focusing on research subjects in a dialogic style was the primary source of information in this study. A paramount issue in the process of obtaining information was the flexibility of the technique used. As a method of 'conversation with a purpose' (Kahn and Cannell, 1957:149), the techniques were based on the 'unstructured interview' (Burgess, 1982, pp.107-110; Burgess, 1984, pp.101-122; Patton, 1990, chap.7). Open-ended and unstructured in-depth interviews based on loosely guideline questions were easily adapted to particular settings and were applicable to respondents' experiences, which in turn helped to ease interaction during the interview sessions. This made the dialogue or conversation process more dynamic and lively, and enriched and encouraged respondents to talk and share more information about themselves, while at the same time their active involvement promoted the integrity of the understanding reached the people's participation through the respondents' active involvement. Thus, the technique used which centrally focuses on groups - so as to obtain members' grounded experiences - was also, in large part, a groupwork-based research approach.

A paraphrasing or recapitulating technique was used in the process of questioning. Probing questions rather than directing, encouraged respondents to share information. When answering questions, respondents made some reflections on their experiences and reasoned out actions taken. For example, in explaining the reason why he participated in a group activity (religious study circle), Mr. Azha said:

> ...I think my main reason for joining this study group is to gain new information, new knowledge...and also to help the study group members. I suppose my involvement is my social obligation to support them...and at the same time I gain some knowledge working together with them. (Mr Azha)

Mrs. Fira voiced the same concern, along similar themes in explaining the reason for her involvement as she said:

> What would happen if you don't have knowledge on Islam...what would happen to us? This knowledge is very useful for our daily lives...I mean I can use it myself, I know what is wrong and what is right...how to deal with people, to respect people. That's why I always attend this class. (Mrs Fira)

On another occasion during the interview session, Mrs. Eton, who is one of the leaders of the Crockery Association, reflecting upon the problem that the women faced before the establishment of the group, explained:

> Hah! at that time it was difficult to hold a 'kenduri' (feast). I still remember, Ali (not his real name) wanted to marry off his son. His wife just passed away a few months before the ceremony. He, like all the families here, are poor... owned only a few bits of crockery, pots and pans, not many...We decided that each household should lend him five plates, bowls, cups and spoons for the marriage feast...From this incident, we, Mrs. Yati, two other friends and I then discussed and decided to set up this Crockery Association. (Mrs Eton)

These are just few examples to illustrate that by giving people a chance to share their experience in initiating and participating in their group activity and by being ready to hear their ideas the researcher was enabled to understand their reasons for their involvement in those activities. Although it is beyond the scope of this article to delineate each of the reasons given on each type of community group or community activity initiated by the people, the study showed that the people had much understanding about their problems and the needs of their community, and as a result of thinking about the problems they began to seek solutions. Thus, the interaction between researcher and respondents in this dialogue style of in-depth interview produced a 'joint construction of reality' (Agar, 1980 c.f. Crabtree and Miller, 1992, p.76). The researcher's and respondents' interactions fused the ideas into one perspective. In responding to the questions, the respondents described the process they had undergone, based on their experiences, and at the same time the researcher tried to understand the meaning within a context that would reflect what had been described.

Consciousness raising

Dialogue involves a two way process of interaction between the person who intends to hear and encourages the other person (people) to talk about their experiences, ideas, feelings, problems, hopes, etc. in a non-authoritarian relationship. The process involves understanding, clarifying, describing and explaining activities. As such, it gives the freedom for people to express their reasoning, expectations and perceptions as to how they perceive the world they live in. It is about giving people the right 'to name the world' (Freire, 1972), that is 'the right to name one's reality' (Breton, 1993) and to define one's own issues (Mullender and Ward, 1991). All these processes developed in the interviewing sessions within which self-reflection and self-realisation took place simultaneously. Both have a consciousness raising element in that by reflecting on the experiences that they had undergone, they are actually making sense of their past experience of involvement in group activity. Consequently, through sharing their experience, respondents became more informed about their actions. This can be seen in the descriptions below.

In describing his involvement in establishing Embun Hidayah (a youth club), for example, Mr. Amsul began to realise that his previous effort was worthwhile, as he said:

> I think my involvement to set up the group last year was not wasted. Now, the parents in this village can see with their own eyes that we, the EH members, can help together in developing their children in this camp (religious camp activity). (Mr Amsul)

This self-realising process, taking place during sessions, generates a form of self-judgement about one's actions, efforts and ability to bring some improvement. With regard to this, it can be argued that the method of inquiry is empowering in itself. It enables subjects to evaluate their capability and to realise that they possess the potential to act for themselves and for other people.

In another session, Mr. Azli who led the Parents and Teachers Association in campaigning for better school facilities, voiced his reasons for changing the initial strategy from cooperative action and close working relationships with the school authority, to firmer action - by demanding and bargaining for appropriate changes to be made at the school. He realised that the new strategy or action was put forward when the former strategy failed to achieve the parents' expectations:

> 'When I saw that soft action didn't work, I called for another meeting. In the meeting, I suggested to my friends that we take signatures of all parents who send their children to the school (Religious Primary School), to be sent to higher school authority...So in the covering letter we expressed our dissatisfaction towards them (the School Division of Selangor Islamic Department) about their slow action...no action taken. We also demanded a male teacher (ustaz), and again we forced them to improve the congested classroom condition. (Mr Azli)

In another instance through reflecting on the same action - i.e. demanding a change for a new head teacher for the Primary School - a group discussion showed that the parents were aware and responsible for the action to achieve their common interest, better achievement by their children at school:

> ...this was my first experience in such a thing. I had never experienced it before but after discussion with the youth leader, I agreed to join his action in sending a petition to the District Education Officer, to show that we, the parents, take this matter seriously. (Mr Sidi)

> ...it is better to do like this...if we are not satisfied we should act promptly, if not, the problems drag on...(Mr Wan)

It was also noted during the discussion that after having realised their action was successful, this motivated them to take further action if the responsible authority should fail to keep their promise:

> I think this issue struck them (the District Education personnel), when we demanded to change the new head teacher...That's why they quickly responded to our request, and promised to monitor the school administration...Let's see, if nothing happens we will fire them again. (Mr Fizol)

Dialogue interaction not only enabled the raising of respondents' awareness about what had happened, what sort of action they had been involved in, or what significant experience had been gained, but it also created and raised respondent's consciousness about the importance of their participation in the group. As more probing questions were asked, respondents became more aware and understood their role in facilitating other community or group members' participation in community development activities, and appreciated their talents and contributions. This can be observed clearly from the illustrations below:

> I admit that most of our members (in the Crockery Association) consist of senior mothers, no young people. They couldn't even read or write. From my experience with them, they have difficulty in writing down the borrowers names or how many plates rented out. They can write a little in Jawi (Malay-Arabic writing). Pity them! I realised their problems...that's why I take the trouble to teach them how to note down the transaction made (who has borrowed what) in a book. If there's no one like me to teach them who else will direct them? We, the ones with the brain, the energy should guide them, that's what I think... (Mrs Anum)

> We, people like me who are quite knowledgeable and know more or less how to organise, to develop oneself, should teach or hand down this knowledge to the village people. If not, what's the use of me being the youth leader here? While working with them, we can also discuss together and show ways to organise an activity, learn together while being involved in the activity. I like this kind of involvement. (Mr Fizol)

The two examples above show that respondents realised that they have the capability to help and facilitate the group or community members in pursuing their group activities. In another perspective, this could also eventually help in stimulating them to sustain their contribution in the group, and thus maintain the group and its activities.

Social learning process

The information obtained from such conversations is not only useful for the researcher, but also for the people themselves. This is because sharing in the dialogue interaction, either in in-depth interviews or group discussions, based on reflecting on the respondents' past experiences, is a shared social learning process. Respondents giving responses to the questions asked, and researcher feeding back the ideas by incorporating them into more probing questions, enables them to speak more about themselves. Since the dialogue takes place in a non-authoritarian context where the position of researcher and the people is a subject-to-subject relationship, therefore with such mutual trust, respect and reciprocity, the information, as knowledge, is shared together. Giving and sharing this knowledge is an empowering learning process. The process involved is not to 'fill the empty vessel' - the 'banking process' or 'depositing' an idea to be 'consumed' by the people (Freire, 1972), which has the 'domestication' effect, but rather facilitates people to be learners in their own world.

This empowering effect was clearly observed in this piece of research. As the study progressed, more questions pertaining to the subject matter were explored, and during the process of feeding back information about themselves through paraphrasing and probing, respondents began to discover and learn that they have gained something from their past action. This was particularly true among respondents who selected and joined the Group Replanting Scheme, in the rubber replanting programme, after rejecting the mini-estate scheme proposed by the authorities. Below are some of the comments gathered during the in-depth interviews and group discussions, which exemplified that they have learned from their action in taking control over the contractors who maintain the plantation, and this was reinforced during sharing information sessions:

> Yes, when I think back about the Group Replanting Scheme I think we, here, made the correct choice. If we had not formed a group like this how could we control the contractors, because we were not strong enough. In a group like this we are more confident to take action on the contractors... that's how I feel participating in this Group Replanting Scheme. (Mr Baba).

> No more worries. Now we, all the committee members (referring to the group replanting committee), are well-versed in our action. Nobody taught us. I think it was our patience to learn from our previous mistake...What did I say to you six months ago? 'Bad experience is a good lesson!'. I want to share this with you. Remember next time, no matter what problem you face, learn from it. The more you can take it, the more experience you gain. Don't give up. (Mr Mumtaz)

From the examples above, it can be concluded that people learned from their involvement and experience, and this was notified and verified in the sharing of information during the dialogue. In this dialogue process they have grasped the idea that through understanding the bad experience, in this case being exploited by the contractors, taking collective action to form the group replanting committee enabled them to regain some power to control the contractor.

While elaborating on and responding to questions asked, describing their experience of involvement, respondents also began to value and appreciate their own actions and the 'power' that they possess. Gaining the understanding that they had acquired such an ability in the course of their actions was a stimulating self-learning process, shared during follow-up interviews and group discussions:

> Yes, actually, as I told you, I never gave up fighting for my people. If this doesn't work, we'll try another way. Now, I'm very familiar with their character (the school authority). We must be firm. There's no point waiting and trying to persuade them to visit us here. It doesn't work that way. That's why we changed our strategy, sending a petition like this is much better. It gets a faster reaction from them. (Mr Azli)

> Now I know, the next time if we want to deal with any government agency, not only with the school authority, we have to deal straight-forwardly with them...[because] if we do it gently, sending letters telling them we have a problem here, they never entertain us, but if we threaten them, they will do something. (Mr Baba)

From the examples given above it can be concluded that enquiring about and exploring the subject matter in its own setting, through a qualitative-ethnographic approach and techniques, encouraged social learning, and this was an educative element in the approach used. The empowering aspects of the approach do not end when phenomenon studied is understood, but the effect of the method used also helps to strengthen people's own belief that they have the ability to act, either individually or collectively. Sharing information during conversation interaction is a process of gaining self knowledge based on their actions. At this point knowledge is a source of power, and this is particularly true when people became more aware of their capabilities.

Empowering research process: the 'products'

As discussed in the earlier part of this article, an empowering research process facilitated by the interactive techniques of data collection is able to raise people's consciousness. Through dialogue interaction the respondents critically reflected on their involvement, and action taken, during participating in various community group-based activities. Their experiences of learning through participating in various group activities were shared with the researcher in the conversation discourse. This further enhanced their understanding about their capability to overcome common problems and to achieve their needs. Resulting from this interaction with the people, towards the end of the research process, as part of the shared learning activity promoted by the approach used, they also experienced some changes in themselves. These changes related to people's growing capacity and ability, and include changes in their confidence, skills and knowledge. These three significant elements represent an enhancement of their individual empowerment. In due course, by being closely engaged in the research process, people were able to evaluate their group activities, diagnose organisational problems, and identify remedies.

Developing confidence

The development of self-confidence was one of the most prominent aspects gained by the members from participation. Obviously, self-confidence is the driving force behind the initiation of, and participation in the groups, as a response to the problems they encountered.

The development and accumulation of self-confidence among community members can be seen from the descriptions below, which emerged after reflecting upon their experiences. The expression and nature of the confidence gained differed between members. Among those who had experience in developing, enabling and guiding group members (the leaders), the confidence they gained related primarily to the process of organising people, and secondly, to the activity itself:

> ...I gained a lot of experience from organising this activity (referring to the My Home My Heaven project). At first, I was a bit doubtful about doing this because it was a big project. But after the first, second and followed by the third ad-hoc meetings with members from different groups, I gained more confidence. Once I was confident, I was encouraged to help my friends to carry out the project. (Mr Kamar)

> ...I have learnt so many lessons from organising these activities. Now I'm confident that we, the women, can work as a group. That's why I never gave up encouraging my friends, young and old, to participate in the study circle. In fact, with the success of these joint-ventured activities with the mosque committee (referring to the religious talks and feasts), I believe in future I would be able to mobilise more women to participate in such activities, or organise other activities that will benefit us. As I said just now, many

younger people are already showing their interest recently... (Mrs Anum)

In the individual and group sessions, as the respondents reflected on their past actions, they were consciously evaluating and assessing their involvement and their capabilities. Their self-confidence developed as they realised and defined themselves as capable and worthy people. Discovering their capability to perform certain actions increased their confidence. Believing in themselves and being able to act effectively, based on the confidence developed and accumulated, is the essence of empowerment. This phenomenon can be seen clearly from the comments made by Mr. Azli and Mrs. Fizi respectively, reflecting upon their experiences:

> Of course I have to believe that I can do this - organising a meeting, calling parents and friends, for example - before starting any action. Believing in yourself that you can do it is very important, if not, you can't go anywhere. You have to start from zero, from scratch, don't you?...My confidence increased as the group began to shape up. It assured me that I could easily guide them as a team in deciding the activity. (Mr Azli)

> I gained new and invaluable experience working together with the local women, organising the Women Smallholders' Association. As I mentioned before, I am new here, just got married to a local guy. Moreover I was worried because the community is divided, but I forced myself to take up this challenge. From participating with them, I slowly built up my confidence. Now I am sure that I can work with both groups, women of my age and the older people, because they accept me. (Mrs Fizi)

Self-confidence, as empowerment, strengthens the on-going capability of an individual to take further action. The connection can be seen from Mr. Azha's effort, who is a member of the UMNO Youth Club, but later led and organised the formation another community project, the bill paying service. This is evident where he says:

> In helping Mr. Kamar and Mr. Fizol to carry out the group activities, I actually did two things at once. Of course, firstly I helped them conduct the projects but at the same time I also learned how they organised the activities. To me, it didn't seem difficult once I knew how to organise people, furthermore, most of my friends share my interests and ideas. Once you are confident you can do it. (Mr Azha)

A similar experience was also portrayed by Mr. Kamar in reflecting upon his involvement in organising two community projects, the Islamic Family course and 'My Home My Heaven' project, as he said:

> ...anyway, I think the first project I had with the community - the Islamic Family Course in 1991 - was a turning point for me. I learned a lot from it and I used the knowledge gained to organise my second community project, the 'My Home My Heaven' project. The first project provided me with confidence, and encouraged me to do the second one. (Mr Kamar)

This increasing level of individual capability ultimately helped to build the groups' collective capacity to achieve commonly shared interests. The confidence gained by group members in supporting and helping to organise and participate in activities, varied according to different groups. These variations resulted from, and reflected differences in, the working practices of carrying out the activity:

> Well, I enjoyed helping Mr. Kamar organising the 'My Home My Heaven' project and campaigning for the TAHFIS school. I learned a lot from them...Carrying out the task that I chose gave me more confidence. When I performed it, something seemed to push me to do more. That's how I felt...That's why I enjoyed it, compared with participating in WI (Women's Institution) activities. With the WI, I feel that I'm not 'free'...I think that's the correct word to use here. (Mrs Wani)

> ...yes, with the Embun Hidayah group, I gained lots of experience handling the Religious Camp for the school children. Although I am also involved in WI, between the two, I am more comfortable with the Religious camp. In the Religious Camp we share the work together as a team. Dealing with our own people here gives me confidence that I am able to contribute to my people...but not with the WI, because although I participated in the essay writing competition, I felt like I was just one of the contestants. I wasn't directly involved. (Mrs Mona)

> I'm really satisfied to be involved from the beginning - thinking about and discussing the activity, then directly participating in carrying it out and seeing with my own eyes what actually took place. I feel it like this. When I'm satisfied, I'll be more confident to carry it out in the future...Not only in the community sports activity, but also other youth projects that I'm involved in...I'm not saying that I'm not confident to carry out activities proposed by the leader, but I would prefer activities that are initiated by us. (Mr Radi)

It is important to note here that the interactive process in interviewing allowed the respondents to reflect on their participation experiences. In these reflections, as portrayed in the above descriptions, they were able to identify and realise that as a product of their involvement, there was a change in themselves. They were consciously aware that they had acquired and developed self-confidence. It was also observed that through this reflection they were able to judge the extent of benefit obtained from the different situations. They understood the limitations and advantages of different approaches that they had experienced, one which was directed by an external body or induced by a leader, and the other which was self-directed. Furthermore, for some members, especially in the WI (Women's Institution) organisation, this process of reflection during the interview encouraged their critical analysis of the activity and the group itself. This critical analysis, sparked off in individual interviews blossomed during a group discussion, when group members and leader shared and began to tackle the problems and limitations. (More on this is discussed later).

Developing skills and gaining knowledge

Accompanying the development of self-confidence were skills developed and knowledge gained. As individuals participated together in the process of identifying, planning and implementing activities to solve their problems and achieve their common goals, skills were also developed. 'Skill' here refers to the ability to do something. Skills are not in-bred, but were attained through a learning process. Acquiring skills is part of personal development.

Identification of these skills was based on people's experiences and reflections, also supplemented by data obtained by the researcher through direct observation of some of the groups' processes in organising and carrying out their activities throughout the study period. This information was also verified and elaborated during the 'information sharing' session with the respondents in the follow-up interviews and group discussions. The 'classification' of the skills, however, is not mutually exclusive. In practice, skills are integrated together; while performing one skill to show a particular ability, others follow simultaneously in a complex interlocking process. Therefore, this 'classification' is for purposes of analysis only. Three types of skills developed among the respondents are identified and examined in this study, namely, organising skill, problem solving skill, and technical skill.

Organising skill

Although the group or activity initiated was inspired by a few members, the process in which they raised and focused on specific issues or unresolved problems together with their friends reinforced their ability to organise themselves, and to form collective action. Experiencing the action process in turn provided them with more knowledge about organising skills. This aspect was clearly described by the respondents in reflecting on the benefits of this action process, as illustrated in the statements below:

> Actually, organising people is something like testing your own talents. I feel that way. I'm happy because the more I'm involved in organising an activity, the more new things I gain...more chances for me to test my talents, my skills...I think if you are in that position, you also can get the pleasure, even more if you succeeded. And this keeps me trying again and again in other activities. (Mr Kamar)

> I admit it was quite challenging the first time I tried it, but as I kept on doing it - calling them for meetings, discussing and deciding together with the members - now organising an activity is routine to me. It's like cooking, you know! The first time you cook the dish it won't be very delicious but as you keep on practising you develop the skill, how much sugar to put in, salt, and so on...Yes, participating in organising the activity is something like creating and developing your own recipe. (Mrs Anum)

Experiences of participation in this respect have an empowering effect. In participating, the individuals were not simply contributing on a 'trial and error' basis. They also reflected on their action. Appropriate actions were perceived as new things, new knowledge that developed and enhanced their skill in terms of organising people and organising an activity. These skills were then used in further undertakings, where they are adjusted to suit situations or the nature of the group to be organised, which eventually upgrades their skills. Here, there is a continuous and cyclical relationship between experiencing participation, and reflection. It is in this chain action and reflection process that new insights and skills are obtained, which are later consolidated when this body of knowledge is 'tested' in further actions, in more challenging situations.

Experiencing the process of establishing a group or carrying out an activity helps to widen understanding about organising an action, as elaborated in the examples below:

> ...Last time I didn't realise it but now I know that organising ourselves in a group like this is good...[because] we can achieve what we want. If we hadn't organised in a group I don't think RISDA would have approved the setting up of this Women Smallholder's Association. (Mrs Maria)

> ...There is a Malay proverb - 'Bersatu kita teguh, bercerai kita roboh' [which

> literally means, 'We are strong if united but weaken if we dispute'] and I believe in this. This applies to our group here. When we are in one group we can organise many things, for example in the case of threatening the contractor, and also the school authority. (Mr Baba)

Through the continuous engagement with a group or group activities, participants were able to understand the benefit of using collective action to pursue objectives. As they experience the process, they learn and subsequently appreciate the strategic skills of organising. As group members sharpened their insights about the importance of organising themselves to pursue any action, they also strengthened their belief in collective endeavours. Although the degree of competence between individuals who had gained and used their skills in organising people (as in the case of the leaders) was relatively high compared with those who just understood and valued the skill and principle of organising, the fact that the latter group appreciated the leaders' skills shows that they had cultivated an elementary knowledge of it. This enabled the leaders to develop collective action with members to achieve their group goal. In other words, by involvement, the members learned, developed and enhanced their organisational skills, which advanced their collective action towards solving their problems or taking action against, or to influence, others.

Problem solving skills

Virtually the whole process of community action examined in my study concerned community members' own efforts to solve commonly shared problems. While struggling to achieve needs and goals, they also strengthened and enhanced some aspects of problem-solving skills. Some of the skills developed are related to solving a group's internal problems, and have significant consequences for maintaining the group and its activity By sharing information with the respondents in the follow-up interviews and in some of the group discussions, they became more aware of the skills they had developed, and this understanding brings with it self-realisation:

> Yes, after being involved in many community activities I can see my potential. Before this I never realised that people like me, a factory worker, could do something for the community...Yes, all this started when I got involved in running the TAHFIS school, and helping to solve some financial problems faced by the school and students in their education, besides assisting in conducting the religious talks... (Mr Izam)

> Yes, I admit I discovered something here. Now I realise that working together in a group is beneficial...we can help to solve not only the problems faced by us here but also in carrying out group activities. I think I'm not too late in discovering this, though I'm nearly 70 years old, aren't I? (Mr Hasif)

> Let me tell you something...I prefer doing work rather than just talking a lot and not taking action. Because the more I do it, the more experienced I'll be. I think that's how I've developed my ability...helping my group when a problem arises, that's only one example. Ah! it's a very pleasant experience once you are committed to doing it. It gave me inspiration to do more once I saw the outcome. That's why I've always persuaded my friends to join the study groups, let them experience what I'm experiencing now. (Mrs Rosi)

As reflected in the statements above, it was through the process of mobilising members, initiating the group or activity, and solving some of the internal problems in the group activity that some members were able to exploit the opportunities to advance their skills. As a process, such participation provides experience for individuals, and such experience generates more insight and understanding of working together and the benefits this brings. The more they worked together the more they internalised and understood this, and more skills were developed. Hence, the experiences gained are the essence of empowering learning for community members.

Technical skill

Another equally important skill which was generated was technical skill. In sharing information with the respondents and in the process of 'feeding back' the information to them during group discussion and in the follow-up interviews, two types of technical skills, namely communication skill and managing skill, were reaffirmed by them.

Communication skills

One of the interesting phenomena discovered in this study was the ability of the community group to organise a strategic way of channelling and disseminating news or information. It was observed that every group had its own informal representative in each neighbourhood. These representatives acted as the contact or liaison persons for the respective groups and were responsible for informing and encouraging their friends on matters concerning their group affairs. The emergence of these skills was reflected in their action in mobilising their friends, drafting invitation letters and encouraging them to get involved in community group activities. The development of these skills once again was confirmed when they stressed the usefulness of experiencing the task they had performed. For example, both Mr. Azha and Mrs. Lina admitted they had improved their writing and communicating abilities, as illustrated from the statements below:

> ...as I told you before, I learnt a lot from this, the more I did it the easier it became. I think, yes, it gradually improved my writing skill. I believe they get my message clearly...[because] most of them who receive my invitation letters are prepared to discuss the matter directly, compared with the last time when the letter did not spell it out clearly. (Mrs Lina)

> My argument is this. We, human beings, are not perfect. But for me, if I do it several times I can master it. I'm able to communicate with my friends just by sending them an invitation letter. Of course, there are some other means - phoning them, for example. (Mr Azha)

> I never got credit from anybody before. You are the first one to recognise our ability here. It is true. That's how we organise ourselves here. Like myself, I'm the representative for this hill area, about 13 houses around here. So, informing friends about the group activities, encouraging them to attend any group functions is my responsibility...As long as the group needs my service I would like to keep it on. (Mrs Fira)

It was also perceived from the detailed analysis that this skill played an important role in maintaining the community groups' activities, and assisted and allowed members to continue and take other actions. Sharing and feeding back information increased their personal knowledge, competence and self-efficacy, and practising the skill also encouraged the cooperative, mutual-help and self-help spirit among individuals in pursuing groups' intended goals.

Managing skills

Managing skills were another kind of competency developed by members in administering their group activity. These involve taking and keeping minutes, managing and keeping accounts and assets. These competencies were acquired and practised as they worked together. The principles of 'learning by doing' and 'practice makes perfect' were shared by them in reflecting on those experiences when they said:

> Now, since I became the group rapporteur I know why keeping minutes

> is just as important as in the government meeting. It's easy for me or my committee to check what decisions we agreed earlier. If we didn't, it would be difficult for us to proceed with our next follow-up action. (Mr Kamar)

> To tell you the truth, before this I had never heard what a ledger is. But now, after five years managing the group replanting account, not to say I'm an expert, but I know what it is about. Once you get into it, you learn it... If you asked me now how much we had spent over the last 9 months and how much is left, I should be able to tell you. (Mr Ibra)

> I'm not embarrassed to show you our group's financial record book, here... Nobody showed me how to do this. I never learnt this during my school-days either. But I tried it myself. I simply followed the examples shown in my youngest son's commerce text book (school text book). I learnt it from here. But, when I went through it, doing it, I knew how it works. Good! It's a real good experience...I apply the same principle, more or less, in recording how much crockery is borrowed and returned from my friends. (Mrs Anum)

Although it can be argued that only a few individuals, especially those who were responsible for carrying out certain tasks in managing the group, could benefit significantly from these experiences, the benefit from one or two people's ability in maintaining the group is shared among members.

People's reflections, as has been depicted, show that through working together people were able to acquire skills and knowledge. This then became new knowledge when they assessed the differences before and after. Together with confidence, knowledge and skills were accumulated, sharpened and widened, as they applied and practised them during their action. As more confidence was developed, people were encouraged to accept and undertake more responsibility, which helped to broaden their skills and knowledge, and, as such, constituted an arena for informal learning and empowerment.

People's evaluation

The continuity and overlapping of respondent's involvement in various group activities enabled them to assess the activities and the groups in which they were involved. This evaluation took place during the sharing sessions in which they identified, defined, and verified their personal development, and it was during these sessions that their self-evaluation intensified.

People's evaluation of the activities emerged gradually during the follow-up individual and group sessions. From a close examination of the information gathered and noted, most comments and suggestions related to working practice in conducting an activity. This was especially true for women who had experienced participating in both externally-directed activities (i.e. WI activities), and community-initiated activities, where they could compare the two. In the group discussion this issue was again raised. Some of them disclosed their regret that too much attention was given by the WI leader to carrying out external activities, rather than focusing on internal activities for the benefit of all members. The comments made were based on their perception and sensitivity to what had been going on since the establishment of the WI, as pointed out by respondents in the statements below:

> ...it's like I said before, if our WI activities focus mainly on helping the district WI, there's nothing much our women here can benefit from them... (Mr Wani)

> Yes, I agree with my friends. Living in one community in a village like this, we need to keep up our spirit of mutual help. That's for sure. But, what I'm trying to say here, if we could have a specific project just for our women, it would be much better. (Mrs Nor)

As the discussion proceeded they eventually came to a point where they identified that inadequate group meetings and poor planning contributed to the low priority given to local needs. From the information given by the respondents during the discussion, it was found that the leader only called meetings to inform and direct/instruct the members to be involved in the District WI activities. Although the group has a 'general' meeting, this is only conducted every two years. The issue of group meetings was raised:

> The problem with our WI group is that we never have regular meetings... Meetings are only held when something needs to be done for the main WI organisation. So, we can't plan, how to discuss suitable activities for the group members...yes! to me planning is important, especially if we could have a yearly plan... (Mrs Lina)

> Actually, I've never had the chance to voice my opinion like this...[because] there is no open discussion like this (referring to the group discussion). Meetings are specifically meant to organise our members for the District WI activities. I think we should try this kind of discussion in our group, at least we could share our ideas - what we need for our own good. (Mrs Mona)

> Yes, I do agree with that. We don't have proper planning, that's the main thing. Regular meetings may not be necessary, we could have one or two, but we must discuss and plan the activity properly. (Mrs Wani)

After sharing and hearing the problems and the needs of the members in the group discussion, the leader took a positive stand and was prepared to take action in relation to planning their group activity, as she said:

> Well, it's easier said than done. Anyway, next year in January we are going to have our general meeting. So I suppose you all can come together...Off hand just to tell you all, in the meeting next year we are going to have a leadership election. Maybe new faces, like Mrs. Fizi or Mrs. Lina can take the lead...In the meantime we can think about any good projects for our group, maybe in sport or other activities...But the main thing, we, together must come and plan, not like the last two years, where only few turned up, how can we plan...? (Mrs Wan)

Among the men's groups, they were more concerned about the 'inter-group problems' and a reduction in inter-group cooperation in the village. Involvement had come to be based on the political division of the community into two camps. By and large, this political division limited cooperative work among groups, and threatened the traditional mutual-help and self-help spirit. The 'in-group' nature of participation and the implication of this phenomenon was translated into some members' worries, as can be seen quite clearly in the statements below made during follow-up interviews and group discussions:

> What I see is that if the activity is organised by the 'mosque people', other group members don't seem to bother much. Of course, they never boycott our activity, but you know, they just attend it, hear the talks (religious)... which is quite fair...But it would be better if they could come and help each other, wouldn't it? (Mr Azli)

> ...four or five years ago we lived in harmony. But now things have changed. Group activities have been politicised. Everyone blames each other. So, what can you expect? Luckily we can still work together in the Group Replanting Committee. If we couldn't, it would be a disaster. (Mr Ibra)

> Can I add some more? For me, nowadays it seems that the mutual help spirit is decreasing...Not like before, where all the village activities were done together...but now only certain groups, certain people join in. The problem is when political matters infiltrate into community life, the whole thing goes haywire...It's only in certain activities, like the religious talks and religious classes I see both groups participate together; the rest I can't see any. (Mr Baba)

These men were aware of the problems. As perceived by them, political divisions or cliques were the central issue, and threatened harmonious community life. Furthermore, this problem had spread across gender, and at least two generations.

Although it was not the intention of this study to solve this 'political issue' which is affecting community activity, having gone through the information sharing sessions with the respondents in small group discussions, opportunities were revealed for them to re-establish and restore the spirit of cooperation. The ideas put forward by potential mediators of the two factions, Mr. Azli and Mr. Kamar in follow-up interviews showed this possibility:

> Well, so far I can see one possibility is through the religious activity, for example the religious talks...because the men and women from both sides can contribute their part...but of course, we need to find some means to discuss this matter. I'm confident I can influence all my friends towards this effort if we really want to work this out. (Mr Azli).

> ...but what I'm trying to do is to establish an educational cooperation assembly. I am going to invite representatives from all groups - the Parent and Teacher Association of TASKI and TAHFIS, the Primary Religious School, primary school, Women Smallholders' Association, Women's Religious Circle, the mosque and surau committee members, and so forth. Any groups that have an educative element in their activity, I will call them. I will contact Mr. Azli directly, that's not a problem for me. I believe he's willing to sort out these problems...I'm sure we can try from here as a starting point to re-unite our members. The basic priority that I will emphasise is education. (Mr Kamar)

Coincidentally, their ideas were quite similar. The opportunity was enhanced by encouraging 'promises' made by members of both factions, although there were some cases where respondents were sceptical about the possibility. These encouraging promises were noted during the group discussion sessions with both sides:

> What is most important to me is who wants to make the first move...I suppose the Village Development and Security Committee members can initiate this. I think Mr. Kamar is the right person...don't think about his age but his capability, he is young of course.

> Let me put it this way, first and foremost, the intention must be clear, no

> political interests. Otherwise we will be back to square one, there's no point. If the main aim is to 'save' the community, I can assure you all here that I'll be the first one to support it.
>
> I'm 50-50, maybe yes, maybe no. But there's no harm in trying. For me I have no reservations. It's better for me and for the younger generation.
>
> I will give my full support, don't worry about that. But in my opinion the best place to start is at the mosque because this is our central point. Many activities can be organised here. To me there's no reason why we can't work together.

In general, both factions' members had similar hopes and there was an intersection of ideas. The recognition by the opposition group of Mr. Kamar's capability, and realisation by the second group that the mosque is an appropriate place for organising the activity signifies this intersection. Building on this idea could help to accelerate the integration process. This constructive agenda, which could foster future community development, had been promoted by the interactive method of data collection of this study.

Conclusion: empowerment as a product of the research process

In order to understand the process of participation, people's experiences, as the primary source of information, were scrutinised. To facilitate the data gathering process, a qualitative-ethnographic approach was used. The interactive and responsive techniques of data collection of in-depth and follow-up interviews, and group discussions, advocated by this approach allowed the people to be directly involved in the research process and helped to facilitate an understanding of their participation in the activities of the community. The conversation style, dialogue, and the interaction between researcher and researched also played a key part in the research process. 'Story telling' (Reason and Hawkins, 1990) was the most significant way used by the respondents to express their experiences and views, and, as such, involves reflection during the dialogue. It was during this reflection that respondents became more aware about what was happening, while narrating their experiences, and in this way, a self-realisation, consciousness raising and self-evaluation process took place. The methodology used also empowered the respondents.

The information drawn out was purely based on what they said, and sharing and feeding back the information to them during the interviews and discussions enabled them to begin to realise they possessed the abilities and capacities to act and to affect some changes in their living environment, and collectively gain more control over their lives. The affirmation that they have developed in their personal abilities in the course of their involvement in group activities was explored within this sharing process, which in turn empowered them more to seek solutions to some of the pertinent issues in their community, including to restore the spirit of co-operation among group and community members.

Thus, an interactive technique of data collection was not limited simply to understanding the processes which have taken place. It developed and enhanced group members' ability and confidence to comment and make suggestions grounded in their own concrete experiences, and, as such, demonstrated an empowering capacity in the approach. The evaluation of the group and its activities was a 'critical comparison-reflection', based on members experiences of participating in various groups. Suggestions which emerged during the research discourse represented members own ideas for collective solutions, based upon enhanced understanding of the problems and issues to be faced.

Ethnographic participative research methods offered an interactive approach to studying people in a group context. From the beginning of the research process, before actually becoming engaged in the real process of gathering data, the 'welcoming tone' from the people signified the credibility that the technique has to offer. The trust that the people showed in the researcher, facilitated by sensitive and interactive data collection tools, encouraged them to get involved in the research process. At the outset of the research process people were eager and confident to share their experience with the researcher. As they became further engaged along the research process through in-depth interviews and group discussions, respondents realised that the techniques had benefits for them. This can be seen from remarks made during group discussion about the method used:

> ...Today, I think there are many more issues concerning our group which arise from this kind of discussion (referring to group discussion). I think it is good to follow the style of this discussion, very detailed, deep down to the root...we can give it a try in our next meeting. (Mr Sofi)

> I just want to add another point. I don't know whether what I'm going to say here is relevant to our discussion or even to your work (referring to the researcher's intention) today, but this is what I feel. After being interviewed,

and today in the discussion, after talking and talking, I realised that we, the older generation, are not weak. Our past action in the Group Replanting Committee proved that we can work it out. As long as we work in a group I think in future we can still manage our own affairs... (Mr Sidi)

...I think we should try this kind of discussion in our group, at least we could share our ideas- what we need for our own good. (Mrs Mona, requote)

Yes, I do also agree with Mrs. Mona. Like I said just now, having group meetings or discussions like this means we can plan our activities more systematically. So far we have not tried it before. No harm in trying! Sooner or later we could benefit from it. (Mrs Lina)

References

Anyanwu, C.N. (1988) 'The technique of participatory research in community development', *Community Development Journal*, 23(1), pp.11-15.

Blumer, H. (1969) *Symbolic Interactionism: Perspective and Method*. New Jersey, Englewood Cliff: Prentice Hall.

Bogdan, R. and Taylor, S.J. (1975) *Introduction to Qualitative Methods: A Phenomenological Approach to the Social Science*. New York: Wiley.

Brannen, J. (ed.) (1992) *Mixing Methods: Qualitative and Quantitative Research*. Aldershot: Avebury.

Breton, M. (1993) 'Partnership and empowerment', *Social Action*, 1(2), pp.13-19.

Bryman, A. (1988) *Quantity and Quality in Social Research*. London: Unwin.

Burgess, R.G. (1984) *In the Field: An Introduction to Field Research*. London: Allen & Unwin.

Burgess, R.G. (ed.) (1982) *Field Research: A Sourcebook and Field Manual*. London: George Allen & Unwin.

Crabtree, B.F. and Miller, C.L. (1992) *Doing Qualitative Research*. London: Sage.

Denzin, N.K. (1970a) *The Research Act in Sociology*. London: Butterworth.

Denzin, N.K. (1970b) 'Symbolic interactionism and ethnomethodology' in Douglas, J. (ed.) *Understanding Everyday Life*. Chicago: Aldine, pp.261-286.

Fals-Borda, O. (1991) 'Some basic ingredients' in Fals-Borda, O. and Rahman, M.A. (eds.) *Action and Knowledge: Breaking the Monopoly with Participatory Action-Research*. London: Intermediate Technology Pub., pp.3-12.

Fals-Borda, O. (1981) 'Action research', Development: *Seeds of Change*, 1, pp.66-61.

Fear, F.A., Carter, K.A. and Thullen, M. (1985) 'Action research in community development: concepts and principles' in Fear, F.A. and Schwarzweller, H.K.

(eds.) *Research in Rural Sociology and Development*. Greenwich, Connecticut: Jai Press, pp.197-216.

Finch, J. (1993) 'It's great to have someone to talk to: ethics and politics interviewing women', in Hammersley, M. (ed.) *Social Research: Philosophy, Politics and Practice*. London: Sage in assoc. with Open University.

Freire, P. (1972) *Pedagogy of Oppressed*. London: Penguin.

Glaser, B.G. and Strauss, A.L. (1967) *Discovery of Grounded Theory: Strategies for Qualitative Research*. Chicago: Aldine.

Graham, H. and Jones, J. (1992) 'Community development and research', *Community Development Journal*, 24(3), pp.235-241.

Greetz, C. (1975) *The Interpretation of Cultures*. London: Hutchinson.

Hall, B.L. (1981) 'Participatory research, popular knowledge and power: a personal reflection', *Convergence*, XIV, (3), pp.6-27.

Hall, B.L. (1975) 'Participatory research: an approach for change', *Convergence*, VII(2).

Hammersley, M. and Atkinson, P. (1995) *Ethnography: Principle in Practice*. London: Routledge.

Heron, J. (1981a) 'Experiential research methodology' in Reason, P. and Rowan, J. (eds.) *Human Inquiry: A Sourcebook of New Paradigm Research*. Chichester: John Wiley, pp.153-166.

Heron, J. (1981b) 'Philosophical basis for a new paradigm' in Reason, P. and Rowan, J. (eds.) *Human Inquiry: A Sourcebook of New Paradigm Research*. Chichester: John Wiley, pp.19-35.

Jick, T.D. (1979) 'Mixing qualitative and quantitative method: triangulation in action', *Administrative Science Quarterly*, 24, pp.602-611.

Kahn, R. and Cannel, C. (1957) *The Dynamic of Interviewing*. New York: John Wiley.

Kolb, D.A. (1984) *Experiential Learning: Experience as the Source of Learning and Development*. Englewood, N. Jersey: Prentice-Hall.

Litchty, J.R. and Kimball, W.J. (1985) 'Analysis of an action research project' in Fear, F.A. and Schwarzweller, H.K. (eds.) *Research in Rural Sociology and Development*. Greenwich, Connecticut: Jai Press, pp.217-237.

Mullender, A. and Ward, D. (1991) *Self-Directed Groupwork: Users Take Action for Empowerment*. London: Whiting and Birch.

Oakley, A. (1981) 'Interviewing women: a contradiction in terms' in Roberts, H. (ed.) *Doing Feminist Research*. London: Routledge & Kegan Paul.

Patton, M.Q. (1990) *Qualitative Evaluation and Research Method*. California: Sage.

Rahman, M.A. (1981) 'Participation of the rural poor in rural development', *Development: Seeds of Change*, 1, pp.3-9.

Rahman, M.A. (1981) 'Reflection', *Development: Seeds of Change*, 1, pp.43-51.

Ramazanoglu, C. (1992) 'On feminist methodology: male reason versus female empowerment', *Sociology*, 26(2), pp.207-212.

Randall, R. (1981) 'Doing dialogical research' in Reason, P. and Rowan, J. (eds.) *Human Inquiry: A Source Book of New Paradigm Research*. Chichester: John Wiley, pp.349-361.

Reason, P. (ed.) (1990) *Human Inquiry in Action: Developments in New Paradigm Research*. London: Sage (reprinted).

Reason, P. (1994) 'Three approaches to participatory inquiry' in Denzin, N.K. and Lincoln, Y.S. (eds.) *Handbook of Qualitative Research*. California: Sage, pp.324-339.

Reason, P. and Hawkins, P. (1990) 'Story telling as inquiry' in Reason, P. (ed.) *Human Inquiry in Action: Developments in New Paradigm Research*. London: Sage, pp.79-101 (reprinted).

Tandon, R. (1981) 'Participatory research in the empowerment of people', *Convergence*, XIV(3), pp.20-27.

Voth, D.E. (1979) 'Social action research' in Blakely, E.J. (ed.) *Community Development Research: Concepts, Issues and Strategies*. New York: Human Science Press, pp.67-81.

This chapter first published in 1996 in *Groupwork* Vol. 9(2), pp.221-256

At the time of writing, the author was a Doctoral Student at the University of Nottingham

Research into Practice Does Go: Integrating Research within Programme Development

Rob Harry,Patricia Hegarty, Cathy Lisles, Richard Thurston and Maurice Vanstone

Abstract: *This paper is an account of the evolution of an integrated and continuous process of the practice and evaluation of groupwork with people who persistently offend, which underpins the work of the resource and policy unit in Mid Glamorgan Probation Service. It covers the historical context, the guiding principles, the evaluation structure and a delineation of the process of implementation which is illustrated by a description of a 'development day' involving researchers and practitioners. In a challenge to positivism, the authors advocate an honest and realistic approach to evaluation and research based on a self-reflexive learning model; and present their analyses and conclusions as an example of that model.*

keywords: *evaluation; self-reflexive learning; culture of curiosity; persistent offenders*

Introduction

This paper describes a model for integrating research and evaluation within the process of developing groupwork practice in Mid Glamorgan Probation Service: inevitably, it is focused on a particular period in the life of a dynamic model, and does not reflect changes that have occurred since the end of 1995. To appreciate fully the value of the approach adopted, it is important to set this within the context of the history and function of the Resource and Policy Unit (RPU) within which the model evolved. The unit was established following the demise of the Schedule 1A Day Centre (see Vanstone, 1993), and during the early period of the STOP (Straight Thinking on Probation) experiment[1]. In different ways both had a significant influence on the shaping of the vision that informed the principles and purpose of the Unit; this influence requires explanation.

During the eighteen year history of the Day Centre (part of which included involvement in the original Day Training Centre Experiment – see, Mair, 1988), there had been problems that are common to many specialist projects. Although it survived for a considerable number of years, changing staff groups achieved only intermittent success in maintaining a viable throughput of appropriate people. Moreover, the staff who had spent varying periods working in the Centre had experienced its positive and dynamic ethos but in a situation of relative detachment from the rest of the Service. Any explanation for this is unlikely to do justice to the complexity of its history: however, some aspects are of particular significance. Firstly, a situation in which a small group of people developed specialist practice led to an appearance of elitism; secondly, the gulf between the staff of the Centre and main stream staff created by the specialist nature of the project contributed to a disparate sense of ownership in the Service; and thirdly, the programmes which evolved owed more to the skills and interests of the current group of staff than to evidence of effectiveness. These factors, in particular, had a persuasive influence on the formulation of the concept of a field-based unit devoted to researching, resourcing and developing groupwork across the whole Service.

At a time when the Mid Glamorgan Service was embroiled in yet another discussion about the Day Centre's future, the STOP experiment was initiated. The concept of the experiment was premised on the notion that good practice should be informed by what is known about effectiveness from research findings. When the decision to close the Centre was made, the idea of creating offence specific group programmes shaped by the lessons of research, and located in the field teams rather than in a specialist unit followed a logical progression.

Accordingly, the Resource and Policy Unit was established with an explicit aim to develop, deliver and evaluate effective programmes for people being supervised by the Mid Glamorgan Probation Service. In turn, these programmes were designed to contribute to the strategy of helping people to deal with problems in ways which lessen the likelihood of re-offending and contribute towards 'protecting the public'. Its objectives are: firstly to work in close partnership with colleagues in the field teams, and to engage with relevant experts outside of the Probation Service; secondly, to ensure that all programmes are informed by what is known about best practice, and contain methods and exercises which research evidence shows are prerequisites of effectiveness; and finally to devise evaluation criteria which enable the assessment of the impact of the programmes not only on the participants but on the organisation itself.

The available knowledge base about 'What Works' in community sentences (for example: Lipsey, 1990; Andrews et al, 1990), and the STOP programme itself, has provided a template for each of the programmes as they have been developed. This incorporates: a method of ensuring the appropriateness of the target population for each group; structured programmes in manual format; a cognitive-behavioural theoretical model; the use of skilled group leaders; ownership by, and support from the field teams; mechanisms to ensure delivery of the intended programmes; on-going training and support for practitioners; and the integration of research and evaluation.

As indicated, the establishment of the RPU in 1992 augmented a policy that continues to develop focused groupwork programmes in conjunction with staff throughout the organisation. The RPU's role in developing such programmes is defined by three guiding principles: Partnership, Effectiveness and Evaluation. These principles have been, and continue to be, integral not only to programme development, but also to the values of the staff involved in such work. A policy document indicating the terms of reference for the RPU formalised these principles, thereby providing from the outset a sound framework upon which to develop and refine the programmes. This has proved to be particularly important in terms of ensuring the provision of resources by field teams, and the sustaining of a strategy that is shared across the Service.

The partnership principle rests upon an expectation that RPU staff work in close conjunction with colleagues in the field teams. On this basis, all the staff - development officers and researchers are involved in harnessing the knowledge and skills of field colleagues in order to develop, deliver and evaluate the groupwork programmes.

Programme development takes place within the structure of programme action groups (PAGs), the basis for which was established from the outset by a policy document which set out their terms of reference (see Appendix). Each PAG consists of at least one probation officer from each field team. They have volunteered to be involved for a variety of reasons: some for more experience in groupwork and cognitive behavioural methods, and others to contribute their ideas and experience from one-to-one work to the process of developing a groupwork package. The intention is that the groups act as a catalyst for ideas; provide continuing support for the delivery of the programmes; create a forum in which evaluation and research is discussed and programmes can be re-developed and refined; and, because of their 'democratic' structure, provide representation and links between colleagues and teams in the

Service.

The co-operation of groups of practitioners in this way to develop programmes continues to access and build upon a broad range of knowledge and experience that has proved to be crucial to the effective delivery of the programmes. Although teams are expected to have one officer involved in the Programme Action Group for at least a period of 6 months there has been flexibility about this arrangement, and this has allowed local managers to utilise other interested staff in their teams to deliver the programmes. Also, officers have moved over time from one PAG to another, thereby facilitating 'cross-fertilisation' of ideas and creating further opportunities for staff development for themselves and for those who replace them. In addition Diploma in Social Work students have been encouraged to take an active role in the PAGs during their placements in the Service. To date, PAGs have focused on sex offenders, women offenders, drink driving, violence and aggression, auto-crime, and the Straight Thinking on Probation Programme (STOP). At any one time therefore, each team will have a number of its officers involved in the PAGs, each being able to contribute to team discussions about current developments.

Administration and Organisation of the Programmes

In order for the programmes to be properly and efficiently organised, the Resource and Policy Unit operates an information system whereby all referrals and subsequent Orders to all the programmes are collated on a central data base (see Fig. 1 below). The system runs parallel to the Services' full data information system and serves a dual function, enabling RPU staff to monitor numbers and throughput regularly, and to evaluate programme process and outcomes (see Fig. 2).

Responsibility for the day-to-day running of all programmes lies with local managers. The PAG member in the field team keeps records of referrals and orders made, and when numbers allow reports back to the full PAG that a programme is viable. After consultation with the relevant local manager, staffing is arranged, following which the programme can go ahead. Throughout this process, administration staff play an essential role as information officers in teams and centrally, ensuring the comprehensive recording and collection of information needed for the process to be run successfully.

Staffing of the programmes has not proved to be as straightforward as we would have wished, as demands on officers' time are so many and varied. For example, when certain teams have been 'stuck' for numbers,

Fig.1 RPU Data Information System

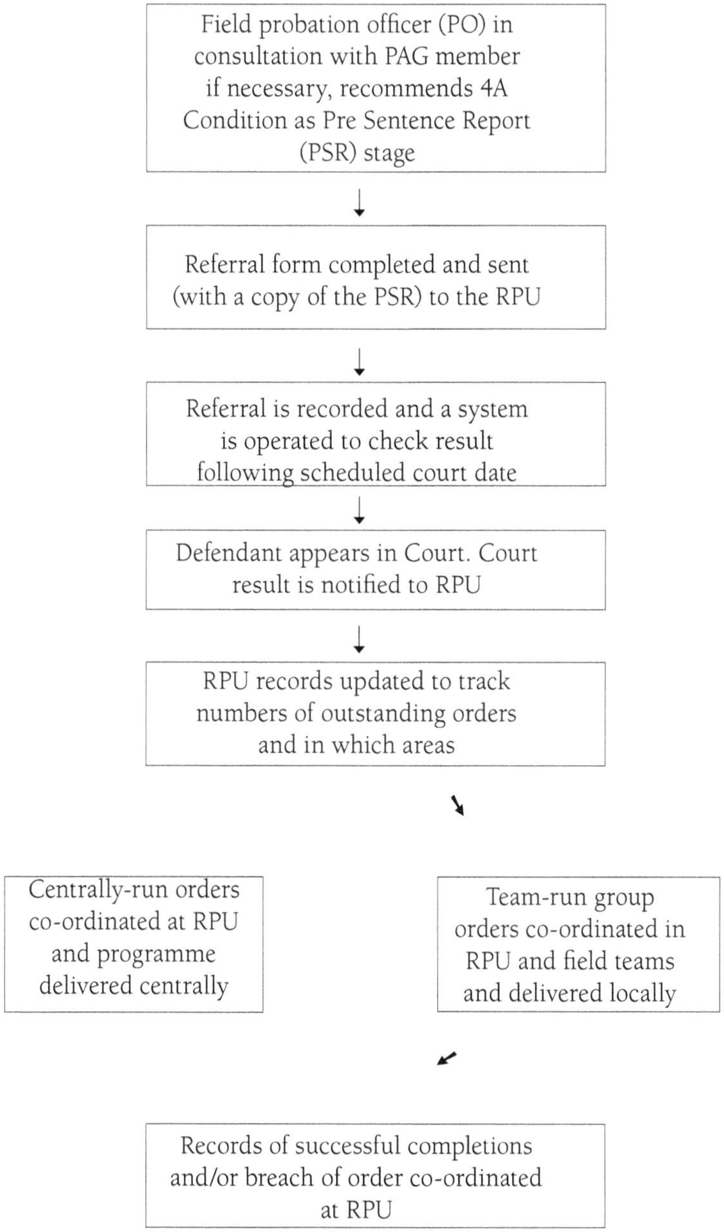

Field probation officer (PO) in consultation with PAG member if necessary, recommends 4A Condition as Pre Sentence Report (PSR) stage

Referral form completed and sent (with a copy of the PSR) to the RPU

Referral is recorded and a system is operated to check result following scheduled court date

Defendant appears in Court. Court result is notified to RPU

RPU records updated to track numbers of outstanding orders and in which areas

Centrally-run orders co-ordinated at RPU and programme delivered centrally

Team-run group orders co-ordinated in RPU and field teams and delivered locally

Records of successful completions and/or breach of order co-ordinated at RPU

Fig.2 Mid Glamorgan Probation Service Programme Evaluation Structure

Evaluative Method	Timing	By whom?
Probationers' profiles	Prior to programme start	Supervising Officers/ Admin Staff/RPU
Attendance and completions	During/After a programme	Admin Staff and Probation Officers
C.R.I.M.E.P.I.Cs (attitude change indicator)	At beginning and at end of programme	Trained Field Team Interviewer
Reconviction Data	During/After programme	RPU/Supervising Officers/Admin Staff
Session Evaluation	During programme	Officers facilitating programme
Consumer satisfaction questionnaires	After programme and at end of order (forthcoming)	Administered in private (organised by supervising officers)
Group interview (sample)	Near end of programme	Researcher (or facilitating officers)
In-Depth interviews with a sample of probationers	After programme and at end of order	Researcher and Practitioner-Researchers
Life history work	As part of content of some programmes	Practitioners and Researcher
Interviews with Probation Officers (group facilitators and supervising officers)	At various periods during the development of programmes	Research and Practitioners Researchers

joint working has been arranged with other areas. Every field team has contributed to programme delivery, with officers outside the PAG working alongside PAG members.

Programmes run centrally are delivered by staff from across the Service. The additional commitment required of both probationers and probation officers in attending and facilitating these centrally-run groups is considerable and evidenced in their enthusiasm. All areas of the Service have been represented in the programmes run in this way, although perhaps significantly, larger numbers of referrals have come from teams closer to the Unit's building. Whether programmes are run during the day or evening depends on information about the employment status of each participant.

An Integrated Model of Evaluation

The evaluation of community programmes run by probation services is most commonly undertaken on a short-term basis and by researchers employed as 'experts'. Where an individual agency might offer a range of programmes (groupwork or otherwise) usual practice and policy is to evaluate these separately as 'one-off' projects. Findings from research of this type, if communicated back to the organisation at all, are not always relevant to practitioners or managers within the organisational context, nor built-in to any developmental or implementation policy; and are thus often limited in the extent or meaningfulness of application. Where suggestions for improvement or change are proposed, this does not always take into account the realities of the working environment, in terms of barriers or conditions of service, which can result in the failure of unrealistic proposals to take hold. Furthermore, recommendations can be left on the shelf if they are not linked to a commitment by the organisation to implement them and a commitment to training, staff development, or further research and monitoring. Moreover, research into practice is rarely given the opportunity to become a continuous activity embedded within the culture of the organisation. The full impact of such a policy is rarely acknowledged, least of all evaluated (see Thurston, 1997).

With this in mind, along with the findings from the 'What Works' research that successful programmes tend to be those with integrated evaluation (Lipsey et al, 1990; Andrews, 1990; Raynor, Smith & Vanstone, 1994; and Raynor & Vanstone, 1996), we have developed a research model which attempts to contribute in a constructive and meaningful way to the development of effective programmes over a reasonable period of time. This is intended to enable practitioners and managers to build upon successes, mistakes and lessons learnt, but without allowing enthusiasm to lapse.

The research conducted in Mid Glamorgan Probation Service on groupwork has two broad aims: evaluative and explorative. The primary objective is to produce evaluations of programmes in order to inform the organisation at different levels about the efficacy of the programmes. This element of research work is mainly a descriptive and evaluative enterprise, and concentrates on programmes currently being run and developed within the Service. The RPU's role in this is to facilitate and co-ordinate so that evaluative work is integrated within practice rather than 'an added extra' or 'an added burden'. One of the aims of this work is to encourage various actors in the process to produce evaluations from their own perspective in the organisation; either as employees or service users. Another is to generate insight and analyses from existing information systems (for example, see that described above). The findings from all these activities can then be fed back into practice development and policy formulation. The work is intended to contribute constructively to debates in the Service, such as those which take place in PAGs, concerning current and future practice through highlighting key issues emerging from evaluations.

It is also intended that research might contribute to more explorative initiatives by providing overviews involving more detailed and theoretically informed critiques on particular themes between and across programmes. Indeed, the information system described above is designed for this purpose of aggregation and comparison. For instance, it is possible to collate comparable data, such as: consumer satisfaction of completers; attitude change; reconvictions; consumer satisfaction of non-completers; and organisational and cultural contexts for groupwork. In order to carry-out the necessary evaluations of groupwork programmes within such a remit, the following research model (see Fig.2) has been developed alongside and integral to groupwork in the Service.

The application of this model is aimed at encouraging the comprehensive gathering and analysis of a range of information, both qualitative and quantitative, relating to the content, process, development, contexts (social and organisational) and impact of groupwork programmes. The aim is to have a structure which is eclectic, flexible, accessible, and durable.

The diversity of methods and subsequent diversity of insight cover a whole range of factors considered valuable for understanding the effectiveness of programmes, including: referrals from courts, attendance, profile information about participants (e.g. previous offending, age, gender, etc), completions, reconvictions, attitude change, satisfaction (on a number of measures), and insight into the experiences of programme participation from both probationers' and practitioners' perspectives. This diversity is built-in to try to ensure that no single 'measure' is allowed to stand alone as an index of the programme's efficacy or value; this is particularly important given the current over-reliance upon measures such as reconviction which are difficult to verify and encourage simplistic and often misleading analyses of programmes and participant change at a local level.

The model has a firm basis in the information system described above (Fig. 1), but adds other research methods and approaches. The intention is to allow for: continuous and regular monitoring of programmes (referrals, attendance, completions, etc); the involvement of field team staff; analyses involving the comparison and aggregation of data from and across all programmes, so that longer-term and broader patterns relating to the effectiveness of programmes can be analysed (for example, in relation to reconviction data, attitude change, targeting of appropriate participants, etc); and the inclusion of current and future programmes as and when they come 'on line'.

Our approach to research acknowledges the added benefits of encouraging a 'culture of curiosity' within an organisational context, and the research model reflects our desire to develop this. Simply put, this approach is characterised by being 'inclusive' rather than 'exclusive'[2]. Indeed, a large proportion of people who are supervised by the Service, and practitioners running and developing programmes, have participated in, and/or facilitated evaluation. For example, research interviews and focus groups have been carried-out extensively with groupwork participants.

It is acknowledged that a research process of this sort, which is grounded in the views and experiences of participants, can have considerable benefits. It can encourage participants to actively take part in decision making in the organisation, and allow for their views and experiences to be acknowledged and acted upon in the process of developing programmes. In this sense, the research work is seen as modelling skills and values which are an underlying part of the programme's approach. For example, cognitive programmes value and encourage participants' skills of critical self-reflection, and research interviews can further reinforce that. As such, the elements of the research model which directly involve probationers in this way are understood as part of the intervention and not separate to it. It is hoped that they provide a further opportunity for participants to review their order, whilst reinforcing a self-reflexive learning model.

This may seem to contravene the 'sacred laws' of social science - especially in respect of 'objectivity'. However, this relates to important criticisms of positivist approaches to the application of research methods. In relation to interviewing techniques, for example, Christine Griffin (1991) argues against a 'nodding dog' approach which involves implicit collusion with everything being said by the interviewee; with the 'justification' that this is necessary to remain neutral yet at the same time elicit information. Not reacting in any way (theoretically possible, practically impossible) might give the impression of passive approval. This can be questionable on ethical, personal, political, and effectiveness grounds. Clearly all this has to be balanced with the goal of producing 'valid' research, and so is a process that needs to be dealt with honestly and realistically; certain tensions and contradictions remain and clearly define the research process as a complex one influenced by a range of factors. This contradicts those who view research as necessarily clear-cut, objective, rational, and immune from social processes or organisational and cultural contexts.

Similar concerns and values are associated with our approach to involving practitioners in research. For the large part practitioner-evaluation of programmes is on-going and routine, and facilitated via Programme Action Groups. This contributes to a dialogue between practice and development, and is recorded in minutes of the meetings. For example, shortly after the production of an interim evaluation report on the Steering Clear programme, a development day was held with ten staff who had contributed to the programme's development and delivery as members of the PAG. Clear aims were outlined for the day as follows: to discuss and analyse the main findings from the research; and to generate ideas and strategies for developing the programme based upon the findings. The day started with a summary of statistical feedback concerning attendance levels, completion rates and profile information on participants (age, previous convictions, etc). PAG members discussed issues arising. For example, they were particularly interested in how age and previous conviction was a factor in differential completion rates and this prompted a discussion of appropriate targeting and assessment. Participants also made proposals relating to the direction of future research and analysis; a number of PAG members, for example, requested a breakdown of feedback and outcomes group-by-group in subsequent reports.

Prior to the development day, a selection of the more qualitative material from the research had been prepared in an accessible form. Participants were asked to analyse feedback from probationers and the probation officers who had run the programme. The aim of this was to engage practitioners in considering in-depth the meanings attached to the programme as experienced by a sample of those who had run or participated in it. This was intended to frame the rest of the day by formally grounding subsequent discussions and developments in the research and the experience of both staff and probationers. The discussion was wide-ranging and prompted discussion of various avenues for consideration in future development work.

A number of issues in particular were identified in the PAG members' analysis of the research, which together generated the identification of one key area for further development work. It became clear from a detailed reading of the qualitative feedback that some probationers were ill prepared for the intensive engagement required of the groupwork. This had caused problems in the initial stages of the group, and was manifested in terms of resistance to the material and group processes, and in some cases was linked to absence and suspension from the programme. Alternately, some excellent work was identified as being undertaken by supervising staff in teams prior to the start of the group. A proportion of both probationers and officers expressed the view that not enough could be done in the time limits of the groupwork programme, and that it was unrealistic to expect the changes in behaviours and attitudes necessary to make a difference to offending to accrue from groupwork alone. Members of the PAG also highlighted that some of the officers interviewed for the research had felt frustrated because it was not possible to go into as much depth on certain issues as they felt was necessary; this was echoed by those present who had run the programme themselves.

A further issue identified by PAG members involved a sophisticated analysis of the data presented to the officers in the morning of the development day. A brief profile of the probationers who had been interviewed had been provided noting a number of relevant details including the length of time which had lapsed from their participation in the group to the date on which they were interviewed. PAG officers were impressed by the 'freshness' and detailed knowledge expressed in a number of comments probationers had made in the research interviews over a year after the group had ended. On further examination and discussion it was revealed that these probationers had been supervised by officers who had a detailed knowledge and some experience or interest in the Steering Clear Programme and the methods and focus of its content. This had been used to instigate further focus on themes from the programme in subsequent one-to-one supervision, thus acting as reinforcement to the groupwork element.

More generally, concern was expressed by PAG members that the programme was seen by some staff as separate to other aspects of probation in the culture of the organisation. One danger identified in discussion was the potential for probationers to experience contradictions between the groupwork and post programme supervision elements of a probation order. This was associated with concerns that programme integrity needed to be ensured across the whole order in order to avoid different messages, methods or focus being employed which might counteract the work done in the group. Consequently, the development group felt that it might be more helpful to talk about a 'Steering Clear Order' rather than single out the groupwork as 'the place for doing interesting and challenging work". It was suggested that future research might be devised to emphasise such a focus on enhancing both the integrity of offence focused work and to increase the effectiveness of the whole order.

Whilst this insight generated by PAG members may seem to be anecdotal and commonsense, the process of engaging officers in analysing research findings in this way did prompt a fresh, critical and explicit focus on issues which can all too easily be passed over in pragmatic and sometimes short-sighted attempts to simply get programmes up and running. In this respect, we agree with Richard Johnson's (1996) assertion that:

> The first and still most important form of cultural studies is to make explicit what we know already implicitly as participants in a culture. (Johnson, 1986)

Furthermore, the solutions which followed were grounded in, and built upon, the discussion of the research findings. Indeed, the morning's debate shaped the focus of the afternoon into a developmental forum. The group decided that a focus on pre- and post-programme material was needed as the next stage in the development of the Steering Clear Programme. The research discussion of the morning prompted and informed a further debate relating to the pros and cons of such work, and strategies needed to implement the necessary changes in practice.

The fact that such a process was undertaken with a group of staff who represented their field teams across the whole Service is crucial. Members of the PAG were able to return to their offices and discuss with their team colleagues the renewed enthusiasm for their work and a greater insight into the effectiveness of that particular area of practice. A further and more profound knock-on effect of the approach is to start to demystify groupwork and research as exclusive specialisms. Indeed, the development day described here should be viewed as part of a process of opening-up practice development and research. The benefits of doing this are wide-ranging. One central aspiration of our approach, however, is that any subsequent proposals for change generated via the processes outlined in this paper are more likely to be met with informed, positive and critical engagement rather than hostility or suspicion. Two years on, we're now reaping benefits of this kind from the work undertaken and initiated on this development day. The proposals made by the Steering Clear PAG in relation to developing pre- and post-programme material were later taken up by the other PAGs for the Drink/Drive Programme, the Anger Management and Men's Violence Programmes and the STOP Programme.

Having a unified and managed system for research and practice development across all these programmes and across the whole Service has meant that research findings and consequent practice developments, such as those described here, are shared, co-ordinated and applied throughout the Service. Moreover, these changes have had an effect on the culture and direction of the organisation. The Service's initial investment and focus on effectiveness - as described in this paper - has been on groupwork. Yet the developments outlined above have shifted that focus properly into other areas of the Service's provision, most importantly one-to-one supervision. It is possible to show how the work described in this paper has acted as a catalyst for this process along with other research and developments which have occurred during the same period (see for example: Deering, Thurston & Vanstone, 1996).

Thus, with practitioners firmly involved in the process of evaluating the programmes they run, it is hoped that this has a number of effects, not least in terms of the following:

- Practitioner-ownership of programmes and research and evaluation;
- Research findings and recommendations for improvements are more quickly and enthusiastically taken up by practitioners.
- Accessibility of findings for practitioners when research is informed by their own concerns and by those of probationers.
- Greater appreciation and knowledge of approaches to evaluation and research.
- Opportunities for improving communication between practitioners, managers and researchers.
- Promoting a 'culture of curiosity' through routine discussion, reflection and learning.

Conclusion

Our aim to co-ordinate an integrated model of development and evaluation within practice is not as yet fully realised. The process of engaging an organisation in change of this type, which impacts upon the whole professional culture, is a task constrained and shaped by a large number of factors, relating, for example, to the local management of resources, changes in legislation and Home Office policy, as well as local management priorities.

Furthermore, it would be hypocritical for us to advocate a system based upon on-going critical reflection and learning, and not to realise the need to reflect on our own practices as development and research workers. As an integral element of the research conducted over the last four years, staff perspectives concerning the role and function of the RPU have been sought. Our belief that such self-reflexivity is essential is justified on two grounds. Firstly, we think it acts as a model reinforcing the importance of being self-critical and responsive; secondly, because as researchers we are always as much a part of the organisational culture as those who we designate as 'research subjects'; and thirdly, because it provides an important perspective on the implementation process so often neglected in research into groupwork programmes in probation and elsewhere.

As a result of this self-reflection we have been made aware of many areas in need of further consideration and improvement. For example, we have found difficulties in obtaining large enough samples to satisfy rigorous research criteria. Moreover, it has proved unrealistic to believe that it is possible to apply a complex research strategy equally and as intensively across a range of Service provision. We have been forced to consider very carefully often subtle distinctions between the different functions fulfilled by monitoring, evaluation and research. In this respect, we have had to vary the intensity of research scrutiny according to the different stages of development that a programme goes through. We have also learnt abut the need for (both senior and middle) management support and ownership in the processes examined above - including inclusion within Service policy and planning. Significantly, we have learnt that when in place, evaluation can provide a basis for consistency in service provision even (or rather especially) during a time of cuts and changes in legislation and working practices.

Nevertheless, what we hope to have communicated here is a system which can create the conditions within which development of practice is grounded upon continuous critical appraisal and reflection, and empirical knowledge of what works best, via an approach which values the inclusion of people within that process.

Acknowledgement

The authors would like to thank all the staff of Mid Glamorgan Probation Service upon whose work this paper is based.

Notes

1. The STOP programme is based on the Reasoning and Rehabilitation model developed by Robert Ross and is essentially a cognitive-behavioural groupwork programme. See Raynor, Smith & Vanstone (1994) and Raynor & Vanstone (1996) for descriptions and subsequent evaluation of the STOP programme in Mid Glamorgan.
2. See David Faulkner (1996) for further development of these concepts in relation to public service provision in the criminal justice system.

References

Andrews, D.A., Zinger, I., Hope, R.D., Bonta, J., Gendreau, P. and Cullen, F.T. (1990) 'Does correctional treatment work? A clinically relevant and psychologically informed meta-analysis', *Criminology*, 28, pp369-404.

Deering, J., Thurston, R., & Vanstone, M. (1996) 'Individual Supervision and Reconviction: An experimental programme in Pontypridd', *Probation Journal*, Vol.43, No.2, June.

Harry, R., Hegarty, P., Thurston, R., Vanstone, M. & Young, C. (1995) *'It gives you a different perspective on life": Interim Report on the Steering Clear Programme*. Bridgend: Mid Glamorgan Probation Service.

Faulkner, D. (1996) *Darkness and Light: Justice, Crime and management for Today*. London: The Howard League.

Griffin, C. (1991) 'The researcher talks back', in W.B. Shaffer and R.A. Stebbins (eds) *Experiencing Fieldwork: An Inside View of Qualitative Research*. Newbury Park CA: Sage.

Johnson, R. (1986) 'The story so far: and further transformations', in David Punter (ed), *Introduction to Contemporary Cultural Studies*.

Lipsey, M.W. (1990) 'Juvenile delinquency treatment: a meta-analytic inquiry into the variability of effects'. Paper presented to the 2nd European Conference

on Law and Psychology, University of Erlangen, Nuremberg.
Mair, G. (1988) *Probation Day Centres*. London: HMSO.
Raynor, P., and Vanstone, M. (1996) "Reasoning and rehabilitation in Britain: The results of the STOP Programme', *International Journal of Offender Therapy and Comparative Criminology*, 40(4), pp272-284.
Raynor, P., Smith, D. & Vanstone, M. (1994) *Effective Probation Practice*. Basingstoke: Macmillan.
Thurston, R. (forthcoming) *The Influence of Organisational Factors upon the Implementation of Effective Programmes*. Oxford: Probation Studies Unit.
Vanstone, M. (1993) 'A Missed Opportunity Reassessed: the Influence of the Day Training Centre Experiment on the Criminal Justice System and Probation Practice', *British Journal of Social Work*, 23, 3, pp213-29.
Vanstone, M. (1995) 'Managerialism and the Ethics of Management', in R. Hugman & D. Smith (eds) *Ethical Issues in Social Work*. London: Routledge.

Appendix 1

Programme Action Groups
Terms of Reference

These Terms of Reference are particular to the following Programme Action Groups; Drink/Drive; Anger Management; Women Offenders; Violence; Steering Clear; Sex Offenders.

1. They monitor and evaluate programme development including research aspects, in conjunction with staff of the RPU. To use the information collated to consider the adaptation and refinement of programmes when appropriate.
2. To act as a Support Group which will facilitate shared learning for staff involved in running programmes. Any training needs identified must be referred to the RPU Senior Probation officer (SPO) for consultation with the field SPOs and the Training SPO.
3. PAG members will be expected to be involved in the delivery of programmes. (It is acknowledged that this will not be possible on all occasions, but the final decision on all group leadership issues will be made following discussion between the relevant field Senior Probation Officer and the RPU Senior Probation Officer).
4. PAG members, with support of the group to act as reference point within the team for all issues relating to the programme. This will include

discussion of referrals, collation of referrals, dissemination of information and maintaining the profile of the programme.

5. Under normal circumstances, to maintain consistency within the PAG, membership should be for a minimum of six months.
6. These Terms of Reference will be reviewed annually.

This chapter was first published in 1997/98 in *Groupwork* Vol. 10(2), pp.107-125

At the time of writing, Rob Harry was Staff Development Manager, Mid Glamorgan Probation Service, Patricia Hegarty was Probation Officer, Mid Glamorgan Probation Service, Cathy Lisles was a Freelance Researcher, Richard Thurston was Research Manager, Mid Glamorgan Probation Service, and Maurice Vanstone was a Lecturer, in the Dept of Social Policy and Applied Social Studies, University of Wales, Swansea

Evaluative study of group work for stress and anxiety

Rhona Birrell Weisen

Abstract: *This paper describes a pilot study of the effectiveness of group work for stress and anxiety. The groups studied were based in community settings and were led by group leaders of different professional backgrounds. The groups were evaluated using the Beck Anxiety Inventory as a measure of anxiety symptomatology, and a 'ways of coping' questionnaire as a measure of coping strategies. The results of this study provide some evidence for the effectiveness of these groups in helping people to deal with anxiety, and suggest that the therapeutic value of these groups may be related to the reduction of maladaptive coping strategies.*

keywords: *stress and anxiety; beck's anxiety inventory; open group discussion; focused discussion*

Introduction

With the growing understanding of stress and anxiety, there has also been a growing interest in developing ways of dealing with these problems. To date, much of the evaluative research of the methods being developed has been concerned with stress management and anxiety management training for clinical patients in treatment programmes, usually with clinical psychologists and psychiatrists (Woodward and Jones, 1980; Jannoun et al., 1982; Barlow et al., 1984; Powell, 1987). However, there are also less formal groups in community settings, generally intended for people experiencing ill-effects of stress and anxiety, led by group leaders from different professional backgrounds. In the light of the lack of evaluative studies of these small and varied informal groups for non-clinical clients this study was carried out in order to gain an overall impression of the effectiveness of such groups as they are currently running.

Effectiveness was measured in terms of whether or not the groups were successful in reducing anxiety symptoms, in reducing maladaptive ways of coping and in promoting more adaptive ways of coping with stressful life experiences. When observing changes in anxiety symptomatology and psychological ways of coping with stress it is also interesting to examine the relationship between these changes (as is suggested in Snyder, 1984). The second intention of this study is therefore to determine whether or not reductions in anxiety symptoms bear any relationship to changes in ways of coping, in order to gain insight into the ways in which these groups are most effective.

The groups

Five groups for stress and anxiety management were included in this study (these were the only such groups, known to the researcher, to be running in the Oxfordshire area at the time of the study). The groups are similar in three important ways: they each include open group discussion of personal experiences of stress and anxiety, as well as focused discussion and activities that facilitate understanding of stress and anxiety. In addition they teach applied relaxation as an active coping skill, with particular emphasis on progressive muscular relaxation, breathing exercises, and the home practise of relaxation techniques. On the basis of these similarities the groups were taken together as 'groupwork for people with problems related to stress and anxiety'. There was no attempt to standardise the groups, since this study, as a pilot study, aims to get an overall impression of the effectiveness of the type of groups described here. However the groups do differ on a number of variables, posing significant limitations to the conclusions that can be drawn from this research. They were groups of different sizes and duration, with varied programmes of activities (which are briefly described below). Also, groups 1 and 2 have elements of anxiety and panic management using cognitive therapy techniques which are not used in the other groups.

Group 1

The setting Cowley Community Centre
Group leader psychology graduate
Co-leader psychology graduate

A nine week course, one and a half hour session once per week; a closed group with eight members (of whom four completed the questionnaires). Each session was divided into three parts:

1. 15 minute general discussion;

2. a one hour discussion of the theme for the session (including facts about stress and anxiety, the role of relaxation, coping strategies, panic management);
3. 15 minutes of progressive physiological relaxation, breathing exercises (and relaxation using visual imagery in some sessions).

Group 2

The setting	Cowley Community Centre
Group leader	psychology graduate
Co-leader	clinical psychologist (weeks 4-8)

An eight week course, one and a half hour session once per week; a closed group with four members (all of whom completed the questionnaires). Each session was divided into three parts:

1. 15 minutes general discussion;
2. one hour's discussion on the theme for the session (including facts about stress and anxiety, recognising anxious thoughts, panic management, problem-solving and goal setting);
3. 15 minutes of progressive physiological relaxation, breathing exercises (and relaxation using visual imagery in some sessions).

Group 3

The setting	Thame Health Centre
Group leader	occupational therapist

A six week course, a two hour session once per week; a closed group with eight members (of whom four members completed the questionnaires); 17 people started the course, but nine dropped out before completing it. Each session was divided into three parts:

1. 10-15 minutes discussion of the theme being introduced in the session (including the role of relaxation in stress management, self awareness and assertiveness, problem-solving and goal setting):
2. one and a quarter hours of more general group discussion;
3. half an hour of progressive physiological relaxation, and breathing exercises.

Group 4

The setting	Witney Community Centre
Group leader	community psychiatric nurse

A six week course, one and a half hour session once per week; a closed group with five members (of whom three completed the questionnaires). Each session was divided into two parts:

1. discussion, including facts about stress, anxiety and relaxation;
2. progressive physiological relaxation, and relaxation using visual imagery.

The final three sessions included more general group discussion (including discussion of stresses related to family, work and social relationships).

Group 5

The setting	Bampton Castle Health Centre
Group leader	health visitor

A six week course, one hour session once per week; a closed group with ten members (of whom eight completed the questionnaires). Each session was divided into three parts:

1. 10-15 minutes general discussion;
2. 20 minutes discussion of the theme for the session (including facts about stress, the role of relaxation and massage as strategies for coping with stress);
3. 15-20 minutes of progressive physiological relaxation.

Method

Participants

The participants in this study were people who attended one of the five groups for stress and anxiety. Only people that had attended a minimum of four sessions of their respective course (including the final session), and completed all of the questionnaires, were included in the study (n=23, 18 females and 5 males; from a total of 35 people who completed the first set of questionnaires).

The control group were members of Acorn, a voluntary sector day centre 'drop-in' for people with mental health problems. All members of the centre were asked to complete the questionnaires. However only those people who completed all of the questionnaires, and who scored above 10 on the first Beck Anxiety Inventory, were included in the control group (*n*=16, 6 females and 10 males: from a total of 33 people who completed the first set of questionnaires). The cut-off point of a score of 10 on the Beck Anxiety Inventory (BAI) was chosen to ensure that people in the control group had similar initial BAI scores to the participants in the study groups.

The study group and 'no-group' control were only matched in terms of their scores on the BAI.

Questionnaires

The Beck Anxiety Inventory (Beck, 1970) is a self-report measure of anxiety symptomatology. Common anxiety symptoms are listed (including 'rapid breathing', 'heart pounding', 'hands trembling') to which the participant responds by indicating how severely each symptom has been experienced in the previous week: not at all, mildly, moderately or severely. The BAI was used in this study in order to compare the experience of anxiety symptoms before and after participation in the groups for stress and anxiety.

A shortened version of the Lazarus and Folkman (1984) 'ways of coping' questionnaire (see appendix) was used in this study to compare the use of adaptive and maladaptive ways of coping before and after participation in the groups for stress and anxiety. 'Ways of coping' are determined in terms of how the person reports that he or she has reacted to recent anxiety-provoking situations; these responses are weighted from 0 to 3 depending on how often each was used: whether not used, used somewhat, quite a bit or a great deal. The original questionnaire was reduced from 59 to 24 items in order to limit the time spent on completing the questionnaires and to avoid excessive disruption of the groups. Items were selected that were particularly clear and which should need little or no explanation by the group leader. Also the items were selected to cover key ways of coping that are particularly relevant in groupwork for stress and anxiety, including ways of coping which are often encouraged as well as those which are discouraged. For the purposes of this study, ways of coping which are usually encouraged were counted as adaptive coping strategies (of which there were 18 items). These included reactions such as: looking on the bright side of things, letting one's feelings out, seeking advice, making an effort to understand and resolve the situation. Ways of coping which are discouraged were counted as maladaptive coping strategies (of which there were 6 items). These included reactions such as: drinking alcohol or using drugs, keeping the problem to oneself, criticising or lecturing oneself. It is conceivable that, for example, 'looking on the bright side' could be a maladaptive way of coping if it encouraged avoidance of a problem that exists. On the other hand, 'keeping the problem to oneself' could in some cases be an adaptive way of coping. It is clear that the definition and measurement of adaptive and maladaptive ways of coping is debatable, and is an area which in itself merits further study.

Procedure

Groups for people with problems related to stress and anxiety were located in the Oxfordshire area. The group leaders were contacted and all agreed to take part in the evaluative research. All group leaders were given clear instructions, both verbally and written, as to how to administer the questionnaires. They were asked to give out the Beck Anxiety Inventory at the beginning of the first session of their next course. The 'ways of coping' questionnaire was to be completed at the beginning of the second session. In the final session both questionnaires were to be given out once more. When administering the questionnaires the group leaders were instructed to tell subjects that these were to be completed as part of a study of groupwork.

The control group completed the BAI and the 'ways of coping' questionnaire at the beginning and end of a six to eight weeks period

Results

Table 1
Means and standard deviations for study group and control on the BAI and ways of coping scores, pre-group and post-group.

		Study group (N=23)		Control (N=16)	
Variable		Mean	SD	Mean	SD
BAI	Pre-group	22.44	12.94	26.25	13.19
	Post-group	12.91	8.06	22.44	11.30
Adaptive coping	Pre-group	19.70	6.56	15.81	4.04
	Post-group	20.44	8.02	14.25	5.94
Maladaptive coping	Pre-group	9.52	3.36	9.37	3.81
	Post-group	6.17	3.46	8.44	4.15

Pre-group and post-group BAI and ways of coping scores were examined to test for statistical differences between the study group and control at the beginning and end of the study. Due to a skewed frequency distribution non-parametric statistics were applied, namely the Mann-Whitney test. This statistic tests for the significance of differences between the distribution of scores, as opposed to differences between mean scores. However, the results of the Mann-Whitney tests do reflect the trends shown for the mean scores (Table 1).

The significance of differences between the study group and the control on pre-group measures was determined using two-tailed tests, since no differences were predicted. Predicted differences on post-group measures were examined using one-tailed tests. It was expected that participation in a group for stress and anxiety should result in a reduction in anxiety symptoms, as well as an increase in adaptive ways of coping and decrease in maladaptive ways of coping.

Results for Beck Anxiety inventory scores

The initial, pre-group scores on the BAI were not significantly different for the study group and control. At the end of the study, post-group scores were significantly less for the study group than for the control ($Z=2.63$, $p=0.004$). This suggests that there was a significant reduction in anxiety symptoms for the participants in the groups for stress and anxiety.

Results for adaptive ways of coping

Pre-group scores on adaptive ways of coping are significantly different for the study group and control ($Z=2.17$, $p=0.03$). Post-group scores are also significantly different ($Z=2.24$, $p=0.01$) and although more significant this result does not offer a useful basis for determining the effect of participation in the study group in view of the initial, pre-group differences between the study group and control. In this case perhaps the mean pre-group and post-group scores are more informative (Table 1); it is apparent that there are no marked improvements in mean adaptive ways of coping scores for the study group or the control.

It may be worth noting that pre-group mean adaptive ways of coping scores are significantly higher for the study group, perhaps reflecting a difference between anxious people who join groups for stress and anxiety and those who do not. It seems plausible that making the decision to join a group presumes there is already a higher level of adaptive ways of coping.

Results for maladaptive ways of coping

The initial, pre-group maladaptive ways of coping scores were not significantly different for the study group and control. Post-group scores were significantly different ($Z=1.64$, $p=0.048$), showing a significant reduction in maladaptive ways of coping for the study group only.

Correlation between reductions in anxiety symptoms and changes in ways of coping scores

Further analysis of the results revealed that for the study group members there was a significant correlation between the reduction in maladaptive ways of coping scores and decreases in BAI scores ($r=0.63$, $DF=22$, $p>0.05$), indicating a positive relationship between reducing maladaptive coping strategies and alleviating anxiety symptoms.

Within group comparisons

When the groups within the study group sample were examined independently there were no significant differences found on pre-group and post-group scores. Also, when groups 1 and 2 (as groups including cognitive therapy techniques in anxiety and panic management) were compared to the other groups, no significant differences were found. It is very likely that the numbers in each group were too small and too varied to bring out any significant differences between the groups.

Initial BAI and ways of coping scores of people who dropped out of the groups for stress and anxiety were compared to the scores of the study group in order to determine whether there are any trends which may help to explain why some people dropped out of these groups. There were in fact no significant differences between the initial scores of dropouts and those who finished the groups. It is, however, noted that all the people who dropped out were from group 3, which started with 17 members; suggesting that this group size may be too large for effective groupwork for stress and anxiety.

Discussion

The pilot study described in this paper provides evidence that groupwork for stress and anxiety in community settings can be effective. There is at least an indication that these groups for non-clinical populations, led by group leaders of different professional backgrounds, are effective in alleviating anxiety and in improving strategies for coping with stress. Participants in the groups for stress and anxiety showed a reduction in anxiety symptoms that was greater than that of people in the control, who did not take part in any such group. Significant reductions in maladaptive ways of coping were noted for participants of the study groups, and also a significant correlation between decreases in the Beck Anxiety Inventory scores and decreases in maladaptive 'ways of coping' scores. There was no evidence of improvements in adaptive ways of coping. Tentative conclusions from these findings would suggest that changes in maladaptive ways of coping were more readily achieved by attendance at these groups than were changes in adaptive ways of coping, and that the therapeutic value of these groups could stem from helping people to reduce their maladaptive coping strategies.

The limitations of the design of this study should be taken into account when interpreting these conclusions; bearing in mind the differences between the groups studied as groupwork for stress and anxiety, the limitations of the measurement of adaptive and maladaptive coping strategies, and that the study group was only roughly matched to the control. In a future better controlled study, each person could act as his or her own control if anxiety levels and ways of coping could be measured some time before involvement in a group (which may be possible in groups that have a waiting list of people for a future course).

This study points to the need to investigate further the way in which coping strategies can be expected to be influenced by participation in groups for stress and anxiety. The results of this study suggest that it may be easiest to effect changes in maladaptive coping strategies.

It could be interesting to see if measures of adaptive and maladaptive ways of coping could help to screen for people most likely to benefit from groupwork for stress and anxiety. The higher initial adaptive ways of coping scores of the participants of the study group suggests that the measurement of adaptive ways of coping could be a potentially useful way of identifying which people are ready to make effective use of such groups. Further study of why people drop out of groups may also prove useful in determining whether readiness or suitability for group membership could be measured in terms of initial ways of coping scores.

The classification of adaptive and maladaptive coping strategies requires further study, and the measurement of adaptive and maladaptive coping strategies will need to be more carefully developed and tested if we wish to explore groups further in these ways.

Further research should explore which types of groups for stress and anxiety are most effective, in terms of factors such as the number and length of sessions, number of members, leadership style and group activities. Evaluation of groupwork in community settings for non-clinical clients will rely on the use of research methodologies that are compatible with the informal nature, flexible structures and varied programmes of these often small and independent groups.

Acknowledgements

The author wishes to thank the group leaders for their patience in administering the questionnaires, and for their enthusiasm in support of this study.

References

Barlow, D.H, Cohen, A.S., Waddell, M.T., Vennilyea, B.B., Klosko, J.S., Blanchard, E.B., and DiNardo, P.A. (1984) Panic and generalized anxiety disorders, nature and treatment. *Behaviour Therapy,* 15, 431-449

Beck, A.T. (1970)*Anxiety: Causes and treatments.* University of Pennsylvania Press.

Jannoun, L., Oppenheimer, C., and Gelder, M. (1982) A self help treatment programme for anxiety state patients. *Behaviour Therapy*, 13, 103-111

Lazarus, R.S. and Folkman, S. (1984) *Stress, Appraisal and Coping.* New York: Springer

Powell, T.J. (1987) Anxiety management groups in clinical practice: A preliminary report. *Behavioural Psychotherapy,* 15, 181-187

Snyder, M. (1984) Progressive relaxation as a nursing intervention: An analysis. *Advances in Nursing Science,* April

Woodward, R. and Jones, R.B. (1980) Cognitive restructuring treatment, a controlled trial with anxious patients. *Behaviour Research and Therapy,* 18, 401-407

Appendix

The following 24 items were selected from the Lazarus and Folkman questionnaire.

1. I tried to analyse the problem to understand it better.
2. Turned to work or substitute activity to take my mind off things.

3. Looked for a silver lining, so to speak; tried to look on the bright side of things.
4. I did something which I didn't think would work, but at least I was doing something.
5. Talked to someone to find out more about the situation.
6. Criticised or lectured myself.
7. I told myself things that helped me to feel better.
8. Kept others from knowing how bad things were.
9. Avoided being with people in general.
10. I made a plan of action and followed it.
11. I let my feelings out somehow.
12. Got away from it for a while; tried to rest or take a vacation.
13. Tried to make myself feel better by eating, drinking, smoking, using drugs or medication.
14. Rediscovered what is important in life.
15. I asked a relative or friend respected for advice.
16. Made light of the situation; refused to get too serious about things.
17. I prepared myself for the worst.
18. I knew what had to be done, so I doubled my efforts to make things work.
19. Came up with a couple of different solutions to the problem.
20. Accepted it, since nothing could be done.
21. I changed something about myself.
22. I daydreamed or imagined a better place than the one I was in.
23. I tried some physical exercises.
24. I tried something other than what is covered above.

Items 6, 8, 9, 13, 17 and 20 were scored as maladaptive ways of coping. The remaining items were scored as adaptive ways of coping.

This chapter was first published in 1991 in *Groupwork* Vol. 4(2), pp.152-162

At the time of writing, the author was with the Division of Mental Health, WHO, Geneva

Anger management groupwork with prisoners: An empirical evaluation

Graham J. Towl and Polly Dexter

Abstract: *In this paper, we focus on evaluating anger management groupwork in prisons. We give the background to, and an update of, prison based anger management groupwork, and outline some of the difficulties of evaluating this type of groupwork. We present the results of a psychometric evaluation of a set of anger management courses (N=50), and finally, we suggest some new research directions.*

keywords: *anger management; groupwork in prison; psychometric evaluation; cognitive-behavioural perspective*

Background

In recent years a number of forensic psychologists in prisons have been involved in the development and application of anger management groupwork programmes. The application of such programmes was largely a response to the needs of prison managers (Towl, 1994). For example, in young offender institutions, young offenders who received high rates of 'Governor's Reports' for various types of disruptive behaviour were identified as a priority group for such interventions. Programmes were applied in young offender settings (e.g. McDougall et al., 1987) and in adult settings (e.g. Towl and Jennings, 1990). By 1991, 15 adult prisons and six young offender institutions reported running anger management groups (Towl, 1993). In May 1992, under the auspices of the Directorate of Inmate Programmes, training for prison officers in running the national anger management treatment package commenced. Since then about 40 prison officer teams (of about 5) have been trained in using the package. Thus we may assume that about 40 prisons have the potential to run anger management programmes.

The approach

The approach is based upon a cognitive-behavioural account of anger. A hallmark of a cognitive-behavioural perspective is the importance placed upon the link between our thoughts and behaviour. This link is applied in cognitive-behavioural intervention methods with, for example, self-reflection and self-monitoring of our thoughts about events. Related to a cognitive-behavioural perspective is a cognitive-physiological arousal theory of emotion. The premise here is that two things are necessary for such an emotion to be experienced; physiological arousal and a labelling of the aroused state. This premise is reflected in anger control interventions with an emphasis upon developing an awareness of signs of increased bodily arousal and practising relaxation training techniques.

The structure and content of the programmes

There are typically about eight modules in anger management treatment programmes in prisons, each lasting about two hours. It is recommended that modules are run at the rate of about two per week. Institutional and regime constraints in prisons sometimes make this impossible. In practice, sessions are sometimes more widely spaced or run over four consecutive days. If there is a high 'turnover' of prisoners going in and out of a prison the scope for spacing sessions is reduced. Staff availability for running the groups can be an important factor in influencing the spacing of sessions. The group requires a continuity in facilitators, shift patterns may militate against this.

The structure of the groupwork may be conceptualised as involving three stages. First, the general exploration of anger ; second, an individual examination of personal experiences of anger; third, the examination, selection and practice of a number of anger management methods (Towl, 1993).

The first two stages involve the facilitators making an assessment of the anger management difficulties that group members report experiencing. At these stages of the programme the facilitators attempt to examine the degree of insight, motivation and capacity for change that each individual appears to have. The facilitators attempt to examine (and facilitate) the group's psychological resources as an aid to helping individuals within it. By stage three the group critically examines various anger management methods with a view to addressing the problems that group members have brought to the group.

Below we give a number of examples taken from parts of anger management modules to give the reader a flavour of the work. The examples are presented sequentially from each stage of the programme.

A commonly used exercise involves 'brainstorming' the positive and negative consequences of having lost control over anger. The idea here is to help establish and enhance motivation for change when it becomes evident during the module, that the negative consequences of a loss of control over anger, by far outweigh the positive.

Another example. Group members are asked to work in pairs and recount to each other an example of where they have lost control over their anger (and regretted it later). Each group member talks through their 'partner's' story to the rest of the reconvened group. Group members are invited to comment upon accounts. The group is facilitated in asking questions such as, at what point was there no turning back? could he have done anything else? were there other ways of dealing with the problem?

In the final stage of the programme, anger management methods are examined in detail in terms of their applicability and helpfulness for individuals in the group. One widely helpful method is to monitor and adjust the things we say to ourselves in anger provoking situations. Examples of helpful 'self-statements' which prisoners have brought up on the groups are 'it's not worth getting into trouble for', 'he's not worth it', 'I won't let him wind me up', and 'I won't let my temper get the better of me'.

For a discussion of the common themes and dynamics in anger management groupwork in prisons the reader is referred to Towl's (1993) Anger Control Groupwork in Practice. This may be of practical use to practitioners who are considering facilitating anger management groupwork.

Evaluation issues

The effective evaluation of groupwork is fraught with difficulties. Two major problems underpin a number of such difficulties. First, the problem of defining and measuring change. Second, the problem of establishing whether or not any change is a direct product of participation in the group rather than the result of other events.

Evaluation methods of anger management groupwork have included; Governor's reports, behavioural checklists and psychometric questionnaires. The establishment and achievement of group aims and objectives for individual participants have also been used as an outcome measure (Towl, 1994).

Each of these methods of evaluation have their own strengths and weaknesses, some of these for each 'measure' are briefly discussed below:

1. 'Governor's reports' or 'adjudications' have the strength that they are a clear measure of reported behaviour often linked with anger management difficulties. A statistical weakness of this measure is the 'regression to the mean' problem. If prisoners are selected for the programme largely because of a very high rate of 'reporting', such 'peaks' are liable to lower whether or not there is an intervention.
2. Behavioural checklists have the strength that they focus on observable behaviour. However, there can be difficulties in establishing the reliability and validity of such measures. For example, those administering the checklist require training to ensure inter-rater reliability of observed behaviour. Also, often individual items on (generic) behavioural checklists may not be germane in particular institutional settings.
3. Psychometric questionnaires provide quantifiable measures of self-reported change, however they do not demonstrate behavioural change.
4. Group aims and objectives may be adequately assessed on the basis of the agreed views of facilitators and prisoners. Just as with psychometric testing, they do not demonstrate behavioural change.

Currently, probably one of the major obstacles to the effective evaluation of anger management groupwork is the very varied selection procedures for group members. Some prisoners present anger management difficulties in prisons and hence are referred to the groups. Other prisoners report having anger management difficulties, or their conviction history indicates that they may have difficulties in this area and they are sometimes referred to the groups. Still other prisoners may be instrumentally aggressive and they in turn may be referred to anger management groups, even though their aggressive behaviour is not necessarily directly linked to anger management difficulties. Thus in this typology we have three groups; those who have anger management difficulties 'inside' (prisons), outside (prisons) and those who are instrumentally aggressive but not necessarily angry.

Each of the three 'types' listed above serve to illustrate the point that the selection of prisoners for anger management groupwork will have critical relevance for the most appropriate type of evaluation.

There is no reason to assume that those who fall into the 'aggressive' group will benefit from anger management groups. Those who have anger management difficulties either inside or outside prison may well benefit.

However, the types of evaluation for these two groups will differ. Related to these general points it is questionable whether or not it is useful to have prisoners from the 'inside' and 'outside' groups on the same programme.

For those with anger management difficulties in prisons a combination of numbers of 'adjudications'/'Governor's reports', behavioural checklists and prisoner anger diaries may be used to contribute to the evaluation of such programmes. For those with anger management difficulties outside prison, evaluation methods can rarely be so focused and are outside the direct purview of prison staff. Psychometric questionnaires may be useful as exploratory evaluative tools for both groups.

One major benefit of psychometric testing is that the data obtained from such studies may usually be compared with normative data. Psychometric measures are probably amongst the most sophisticated of self-report methods. One major criticism of self-report measures is the response bias problem.

Two factors which may impact on response bias effects are what may be termed 'contingency-explicitness' and 'sanction scope'. For example, in a prison setting a prisoner may be informed that if he attends x group then a 'good report' will result which may very well contribute to his early release. In this example the contingency, group attendance with early release, is very explicit, early release is also a very positive sanction.

In practice, it is probably axiomatic to state that engagement in constructive structured activities in prisons, by prisoners, is generally positively sanctioned. Thus it is reasonable to suppose that the prisoners engaged in our groupwork may well have had a general expectancy that this was so. However, it was made clear to (potential) candidates for our groups that their individual psychometric scores would be confidential. The contingencies within the prison may have resulted in a bias to 'motivate' prisoners to attend. However, crucially, psychometric scores were not linked with positive (or negative) sanctions.

Below we outline the results of an exploratory evaluation of an anger management group using the State Trait Anger Expression Inventory (STAXI).

A psychometric evaluation of anger control groupwork using the State Trait Anger Expression Inventory

STAXI data was collected over nine anger management courses run between February 1991 and September 1993 (8 courses were run in a security category C prison and 1 at a security category B prison). All courses were co-facilitated by a Psychologist and a Probation Officer. Prisoners attending the courses were asked to complete the STAXI prior to, and 7 to 14 days after completion of the course. A further, later, follow-up would have been desirable but regrettably not feasible. The STAXI was used as a measure to assess self-reported changes in the prisoners' experience and expression of anger. Approximately a hundred prisoners were referred for the groupwork, about 40 of these were deemed unsuitable or, for logistical reasons, unable to attend for the full programme. Of the remaining 60 prisoners who commenced the groups, 50 prisoners completed the programme and filled in 'before' and 'after' STAXIs. Only prisoners who had attended the course and completed both 'before' and 'after' measures were included in this evaluation (N=50).

The STAXI

The STAXI consists of 44 items, forming six scales and two sub-scales to measure the experience and expression of anger.

The experience of anger, as measured by the STAXI, is conceptualised as having two major components:

1. State anger - defined as an emotional state marked by subjective feelings which vary in intensity over time, according to frustration experienced or perceived injustice, attack or unfair treatment. The STAXI includes a 10 item 'state anger' scale which measures the intensity of angry feelings at a particular time.
2. Trait anger - defined as the disposition to perceive a wide range of situations as annoying or frustrating, with a tendency to respond to these situations with elevations in state anger. A 10 item 'trait anger' scale measures individual differences in the disposition to experience anger. This scale has two sub-scales:
   a. Angry temperament - a four item sub-scale measuring the general propensity to experience and express anger without specific provocation.
   b. Angry reaction - a four item sub-scale measuring individual differences in the disposition to express anger when criticised or treated unfairly by others.

Anger expression, as measured by the STAXI, is conceptualised as having three key components:

1. Anger-in - which involves anger directed inward (i.e. anger which is

held in or suppressed). The eight item 'anger-in' scale measures the frequency with which angry feelings are suppressed.

2. Anger-out - which involves the expression of anger towards people or objects in the environment. The 8 item 'anger-out' scales measures the frequency with which angry feelings are expressed in this way.
3. Anger control - which refers to individual differences in the extent to which attempts are made to control the expression of anger. The eight item 'anger control' scale measures the frequency with which an individual attempts to control their expression of anger.

The STAXI also consists of an 'Anger Expression' scale which is based on the responses to the 'anger-in', 'anger-out' and 'anger control' scales. This scale provides a general index of the frequency that anger is expressed, regardless of the direction of expression (Spielberger, 1988).

At present, there is no normative STAXI data from the general British prison population available to assist in the interpretation of the STAXI scores. The STAXI professional manual (Spielberger, 1988) provides normative data based on the responses of American male prisoners. Means, standard deviations and tables of percentiles derived from the frequency distributions of the normative sample are provided. We feel that these are the most appropriate set of normative data available, although we would add a cautionary caveat insofar as there will be cultural differences between the two groups.

Results

In the present evaluation, means and standard deviations were calculated for the pre and post course scores, on each of the six scales and two sub-scales. For details, see Table 1, which also provides the means and standard deviations from the normative data. A t-test for related samples was carried out on the scores for each of the STAXI scales to determine whether there were any significant differences between the pre and post-course scores. Table 2 shows the value and the level of significance for each of these analyses.

Data analyses

Individuals who score above the 75th percentile on the STAXI scales are more likely to experience anger to the extent that it may interfere

TABLE 1
DESCRIPTIVE STATISTICS: STAXI -NORMATIVE DATA AND PRE AND POST-COURSE DATA

SCALE	NORMATIVE DATA MEAN	NORMATIVE DATA STANDARD DEVIATION	PRE-COURSE (N = 50) MEAN	PRE-COURSE (N = 50) STANDARD DEVIATION	POST-COURSE (N = 50) MEAN	POST-COURSE (N = 50) STANDARD DEVIATION
STATE ANGER	15.06	6.55	13.14	5.95	11.34	3.08
TRAIT ANGER	21.66	6.71	23.82	7.01	20.38	7.01
ANGRY TEMPERAMENT	7.25	3.27	9.74	3.20	8.40	3.01
ANGRY REACTION	9.59	3.02	9.26	3.51	8.36	3.23
ANGER-IN	18.06	4.61	18.98	4.47	17.54	5.21
ANGER-OUT	16.52	4.96	19.40	5.34	18.32	4.60
ANGER CONTROL	24.79	4.98	17.26	5.44	19.38	6.23
ANGER EXPRESSION	NOT AVAILABLE		37.10	11.16	32.50	11.11

TABLE 1
DESCRIPTIVE STATISTICS: STAXI -NORMATIVE DATA AND PRE AND POST-COURSE DATA

	NORMATIVE DATA		PRE-COURSE (*N* = 50)		POST-COURSE (*N* = 50)	
SCALE	MEAN	STANDARD DEVIATION	MEAN	STANDARD DEVIATION	MEAN	STANDARD DEVIATION
STATE ANGER	15.06	6.55	13.14	5.95	11.34	3.08
TRAIT ANGER	21.66	6.71	23.82	7.01	20.38	7.01
ANGRY TEMPERAMENT	7.25	3.27	9.74	3.20	8.40	3.01
ANGRY REACTION	9.59	3.02	9.26	3.51	8.36	3.23
ANGER-IN	18.06	4.61	18.98	4.47	17.54	5.21
ANGER-OUT	16.52	4.96	19.40	5.34	18.32	4.60
ANGER CONTROL	24.79	4.98	17.26	5.44	19.38	6.23
ANGER EXPRESSION	NOT AVAILABLE		37.10	11.16	32.50	11.11

TABLE 3
DESCRIPTIVE STATISTICS FOR GROUPS 1 & 2 ON STAXI SCALES: PRE AND POST-COURSE

	PRE-COURSE				POST-COURSE			
	GROUP 1 < 75TH PERCENTILE		GROUP 2 > 75TH PERCENTILE		GROUP 1 < 75TH PERCENTILE		GROUP 2 > 75TH PERCENTILE	
SCALE	MEAN	STANDARD DEVIATION	MEAN	STANDARD DEVIATION	MEAN	STANDARD DEVIATION	MEAN	STANDARD DEVIATION
STATE ANGER	11.29	1.81	26.67	7.91	10.89	2.47	14.67	4.68
TRAIT ANGER	19.54	3.63	32.12	3.80	18.09	4.52	26.00	7.44
ANGRY TEMPERAMENT	6.65	1.56	11.73	2.20	6.55	1.75	9.63	3.04
ANGRY REACTION	7.21	1.81	13.62	1.87	7.32 =	_ 2.53	10.56	3.64
ANGER-IN	15.55	2.56	23.00	2.39	14.59	4.31	21.00	3.87
ANGER-OUT	15.12	2.42	23.68	3.81	15.96	3.43	20.72	4.38

with their optimal functioning. Individuals scoring between the 25th percentile and 75th percentile may be considered to be within the 'normal' range (Spielberger, 1988).

Separate analyses were carried out for those prisoners scoring between the 25th and 75th percentile (Group 1), and those scoring above the 75th percentile (Group 2) for each of the STAXI scales for which percentiles are available (state anger, trait anger, angry temperament, angry reaction, anger-in and anger-out). Table 3 provides the means and standard deviations for groups 1 and 2 on each of these scales, pre and post-course.

Table 2 shows the T value and level of significance derived from tests carried out separately on groups 1 and 2 for each of the scales.

Discussion of results

The results will be discussed for each individual scale:

State anger

The results indicate a significant reduction in the intensity of angry feelings which prisoners were experiencing following the course. However, the breakdown of analyses according to percentiles indicates that the significance of the decrease is accounted for by the scores of the six prisoners, falling above the 75th percentile before the course. It is possible that these six prisoners' angry feelings were situationally determined and their situation had changed between 'test' times. Alternatively, their high scores may reflect chronic anger which they were managing more effectively after the course. To what extent the changes were linked to the course cannot be firmly established. The finding that there was no significant decrease in the scores for the majority of prisoners may be a consequence of there being little opportunity for the scores to decrease (i.e. a large proportion (N=23) scored the minimum for this scale both 'before' and 'after' the course).

Trait anger

The results indicate a significant reduction in the scores for prisoners scoring both above and below the 75th percentile (although the level of significance is higher for prisoners scoring above the 75th percentile). It may be that the programme, on a general level, helped prisoners to assess and deal more effectively with anger provoking situations and their experience of anger and frustration within these situations.

For the two sub-scales of this scale, significant reductions in the scores of the whole group were found:

1. Angry temperament - this sub-scale changed significantly for group 2 but not group 1. The course may have helped some prisoners who had a propensity to experience and express anger without specific provocation, by increasing their understanding of their own anger and its manifestations.
2. Angry reaction - This sub-scale changed significantly for group 2 but not group 1: for prisoners who were highly sensitive to criticism or perceived affronts, the course's cognitive focus on evaluating and dealing with difficult situations and considering the consequences of any actions may have reduced the likelihood of them expressing anger in such situations.

Anger-in

The results indicate a significant reduction in the 'anger-in' scores, whether or not they fell above the 75th percentile. The emphasis within the programme that anger is a 'normal' emotion and can be expressed constructively with assertive behaviour, may have contributed to the general reduction in scores.

Anger-out

Although there was not a significant decrease in the 'anger-out' scores overall, there was a significant reduction in scores falling above the 75th percentile. It appears the course was helpful for those prisoners who frequently expressed anger in aggressive behaviour, in reducing the frequency of this behaviour.

Anger control

A significant increase in 'anger control' scores overall was found, indicating prisoners were investing more energy into monitoring and preventing their experience and expression of anger. Unfortunately, it was not possible to breakdown the analyses according to the score percentiles, as normative data for this scale and the 'anger-expression' scale was not available.

Anger expression

Unsurprisingly (in view of the results from the 'anger-in', 'anger-out' and 'anger control' scale scores) there was a significant reduction in the prisoners' scores on this scale (i.e. the frequency with which prisoners reported expressing their anger decreased).

Some limitations of our evaluation

The STAXI is a self-report measure rather than a behavioural measure. In other words, our evaluation is based on what people say that they do, rather than what we have observed them doing. Self-report measures are frequently criticised for this reason. Behavioural checklist models also rely on similar levels of observations, but of others rather than the self. Our interpretation of the results is limited by a number of factors: first, the lack of control data and normative data derived from the UK prison population. Second, the lack of follow-up data or information on offence type, age, length of sentence, reason for attending course and nature of perceived difficulties for those prisoners included in the evaluation. Thirdly, our lack of information on prisoners who did not complete the course or declined to complete the STAXI.

Conclusions

These results add to the growing body of psychometric evidence to suggest that cognitive behaviourally based anger management groupwork interventions in prisons do work. However, our conclusions can only be tentative in the light of the manifold conceptual complexities and methodological difficulties associated with the effective evaluation of anger management groupwork. Inevitably in the prison environment, researchers are limited in the methodological purity of their research. Our results may be a statistical artefact of the use of multiple t-tests. We believe that our results are encouraging, but that further data analyses may be warranted. Indeed, if we can improve future data sets, opportunities for more comprehensive multi-variate analyses exist and may well prove fruitful.

We find these results promising but inconclusive, and below we make a number of recommendations about research design for future evaluations.

Recommendations for future evaluative research

1. There is a need to conduct a qualitative evaluation of the experiences of prisoners in relation to their anger before and after the interventions.
2. There is a need to take biographic information on prisoners who participate e.g. age, offence type.
3. There is a need to establish behavioural outcomes of anger management interventions.

Point number one is important because it may help us to understand what is 'working' in the interventions. Point number two may help us in understanding who it is working for. Finally, point number three would give us considerably increased confidence that participants had got to grips with effectively controlling their anger.

Note

The views expressed in this paper are those of the authors and they may not necessarily represent the views of the prison service.

References

Copestake, S. (1993) *An Evaluation of the National Anger Management Programme* (of the Prison Service). Unpublished MSc Research Project. From Prison Service Psychology, Home Office, Prison Department.

Law, K. (1993) *Use of Behaviour Monitoring Checklists in the Evaluation of Anger Management Course.* Unpublished Research Paper. From Prison Service Psychology, Home Office, Prison Department.

McDougall, C., Thomas, M. and Wilson, J. (1987) 'Cognitive control of anger' in McGurk, B., Thornton, D. and Williams, M. (eds.) *Applying Psychology to Imprisonment.* London: HMSO.

Novaco, R.W. (1975) *Anger Control: The Development and Evaluation of an Experimental Treatment.* Lexington, Mass: D.C. Heath.

Novaco, R.W. (1985) *Anger, Stress and Coping with Provocation; An Instructional Manual.* University of California, Irvine.

Spielberger, C.D. (1988) *State Trait Anger Expression Inventory: STAXI Professional Manual.* Psychological Assessment Resources, Inc. Florida, USA.

Towl, G.J. and Jennings, M. (1990) *An Anger Control Course at HMP. Highpoint: DPS Series 2, 177,* Home Office, Prison Service.

Towl, G.J. (1993) 'Anger Control Groupwork in Practice' in Clark, N.K. and Stephenson, G.M. (eds.) *Children, Evidence and Procedure. Issues in Criminological and Legal Psychology, No 20.* Leicester: British Psychological Society, DCLP.

Towl, G.J. (1994) 'Anger control groupwork in prisons' in *Perspectives On Violence.* The Howard League, Quartet Publishers.

This chapter was first published in 1994 in *Groupwork* Vol. 7(3), pp.256-269

At the time of writing, both authors were Forensic Psychologists with the Prison Service

Researching our own practice: Single system design for groupwork

Paul Johnson, Aaron Beckerman and Charles Auerbach

***Abstract**: Exploring the effectiveness of our own work is emphasized in this paper. We suggest that the method of monitoring practice through the Single System Design (SSD) is particularly suitable for groupwork. The principles underlying this method are then explained and its advantages are listed. Also - a number of examples are offered to show how SSD can be incorporated into groupwork practice. The practitioner's view, rather than the opinions of researchers, is vital in this method and, from this angle we show how accountability and responsibility of the practitioner to the client, the group, the agency and the public can be addressed.*

Keywords: *single system design; practitioner as researcher; process and outcome; graphic presentation*

Introduction

Over the course of our social work careers, all three authors can recall instances when they wanted to demonstrate their work to a colleague, supervisor, administrator etc. 'Why couldn't she or he have been there to witness the work I did? If only they had heard what Johnny said! What a productive meeting!'

The first paid position for one of the authors, as a freshly minted professional social worker, was as a group worker with four different groups in a 52-bed intermediate care facility for dual diagnosed clients: Health Group; Socialization group; Client Counseling Group and a Neighborhood Advisory Group. Ongoing funding depended on documentation indicating that stated goals had been met within the allotted time period.

Classical evaluation methods such as pre and post testing instruments created by the funding agencies were used to measure group movement. In some of the studies, process records were also used. While we provided the information requested by different agencies, there was general agreement among the staff that our knowledge of the impact of the programs on the group members was vague and incomplete. In addition, regardless of outcome, we were unable to satisfactorily attribute or explain the outcome as related to the intervention of the practitioner/ social worker.

A great deal has changed for us since then. In this paper we shall explain and demonstrate the ways we explore process and outcome now with the help of a simple method that does both. Perhaps it may help if we begin with three examples.

Three examples

Example 1: The attendance problem

In the Social Work BA programme at Lehman College (Bronx, New York, USDA), SSD is simultaneously introduced into the practice class and the field seminar. This approach supports and reinforces the relationship between practice and research.

In the field seminar, the students are able to talk about the difficulties they are confronting in their respective placement. This setting also enables the student to look critically and reflectively at their role as practitioners. Here are three examples of students using the SSD:

Two students, Vera and Cathy, were co-leaders of an adolescent girls' group. While the stated function of the group was to address issues of sexuality, the immediate problem was poor and sporadic attendance. With an enrolment of 15 members, attendance at the first six weeks of the program ranged between five and six members. In addition, only three members attended the first five meetings. Weeks 1-6 was regarded as the 'Baseline Period' of the study.

The Baseline Period can be regarded as a period of exploration – a data gathering period which helps the practitioner to begin to understand the dimensions of the problem and to consider ways of intervening. The initial hypothesis is formulated during the Baseline Period i.e., the specific problem and specific intervention(s) are defined.

Intervention Period: Weeks 7-10.

The 'Intervention Period' refers to those group sessions during which the workers deliberately alter their involvement in the group in a direction which they consider helpful. During this period, the workers intervene in the process intentionally to see if the group process can be influenced in the chosen direction.

In examining the Baseline Period, the group workers recognized that most of the Baseline Period meetings had focused on issues of sexuality, with minimum attention to the relationship between group members, or between the group members and the group workers. Their working hypothesis was that with the development of a comfortable relationship between the group members, attendance will increase and the group will be more ready to address the loaded issue of sexuality.

In the Intervention Period, the group workers increased their contact with the members between meetings, helped the group to establish a membership phone tree, and in the meetings promoted discussion about the nature of the relationships between the members, as well as between the members and the group workers. The underlying objective was to create a safe environment in which group members could begin to trust one another, and risk talking about sexuality. The result was impressive: attendance increased from five or six in the Baseline Period, to 10 to 15 members in the Intervention Period.

One of the most important advantages of Single System Design (SSD) is the ability to visualize the results of your work. In our experience as research teachers, students have often commented on the value of these graphs in explaining their work to colleagues, including non-social workers, in the field work placement. It can, under certain circumstances, be very helpful to clients.

Statistics can be helpful in interpreting the findings. For the first example (study no. 1), the mean attendance in the Baseline Period was 4.60 compared to 10.40 in the Intervention Period. This is more than a 100.0% increase in attendance in the Intervention Period compared to the Baseline Period.

Using a statistical test, the Celeration Line Technique, the likelihood of the difference of means (attendance), between the baseline and intervention period is only 1 in a 100 times by chance (<.01). In research terms, the findings are statistically significant.

Once the raw data has been entered, SSD graphs, charts and statistics are a click away on SINGWIN. In this case, in terms of attendance, Vera and Cathy achieve both practical and statistical significance. Vera and Cathy prepared a graph illustrating attendance changes in the group (Figure 1).

It is important to note that this was an SSD groupwork research study conducted by undergraduate students in their practice class rather than by accomplished researchers.

Figure 1. Female adolescents attending health group

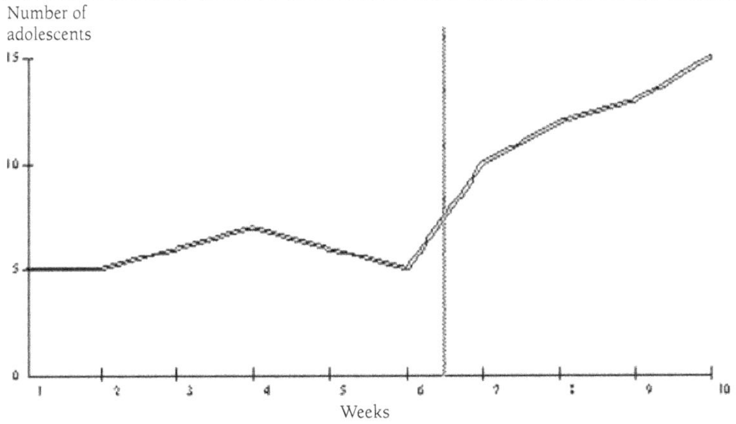

Figure 2. Participants who spoke at weekly VA meeting

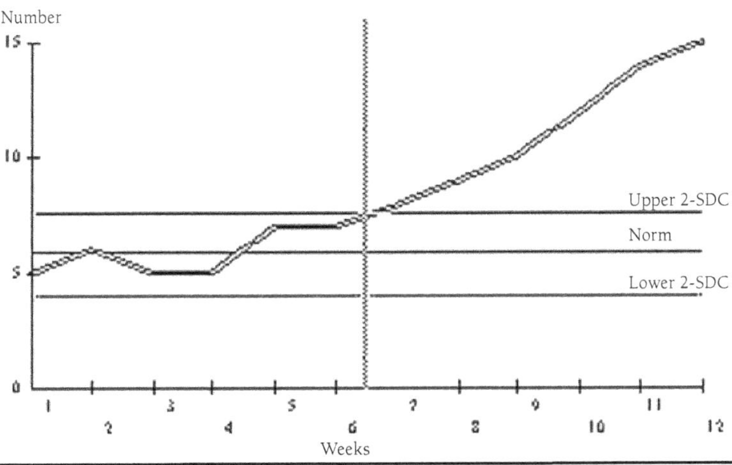

Example 2: Measuring Membership Verbalization.

The student Bert was on a War Veterans Administration placement, working with men who were in a shelter program. When meeting individually with Bert, many shelter residents spoke about the same set of problems: substance abuse, being unemployed, financial problems, homelessness, and little or no contact with their respective biological families. Since the veterans were raising similar problems, Bert reasoned that it would be a good idea to hold weekly group meetings where residents could raise these issues, and perhaps be of help to each other.

However, during the baseline period (Weeks 1-6) out of 15 individuals, the same group of five to seven veterans did all the talking. Bert was interested in trying to get the non-verbal members to join the group conversation.

Intervention Period: (Weeks 7-12)

Bert used a series of interventions to involve 'the silent majority' to become verbally active in the group meetings:

- *Intervention no.1:* Bert raised the problem of the 'silent majority' with two of the indigenous leaders who raised the issue at the next meeting. . The indigenous leaders began to encourage some of the 'silent majority' to speak at the meetings.
- *Intervention no.2:* When spoken to by a veteran outside of the meeting, Bert made it a point to urge the veteran to bring up the issue at the next meeting. As a result, a number of the 'silent majority' veterans began to participate verbally in the group meetings.
- *Intervention no.3:* Depending on the topic, Bert looked for opportunities to call upon some of the 'silent majority' to participate in the discussion. This could also take the form of assigning one or two members to bring up and lead the discussion on a specific issue.
- *Intervention no.4:* William Schwartz (1961) wrote about the importance of the group worker 'lending a vision' to the group. Bert would often talk to the group about the ability to listen to each other. Members were surprised to learn how many problems they shared with one another.

In time, some of the street-smart veterans offered suggestions as to how to negotiate the different systems, e.g., social welfare, veterans' administration, and housing, etc. This contributed to the cohesion of the group and increased morale of the group members.

In Figure 2, we can see the increase in the number of individuals who speak in the intervention period compared to the number of those who spoke during the Baseline Period. The mean score of numbers of veterans who spoke in the Baseline Period is 5.83 compared to 11.33 in the intervention period, which is almost a 100.0% increase.

The above statistical test is called a Two Standard Deviation Band Test (2SDB). The 2SDB Test in Graph 1 indicated that the difference in the number of veterans who spoke at the meetings, during the Baseline Period, compared to the number of veterans who spoke during the Intervention Period could only have happened by chance 5 in 100 times

(<.05), which is statistically significant.

The two SSD groupwork studies undertaken by undergraduate social work students Vera and Cathy, and by Bert, begin to indicate ways of conducting SSD group work research. In both cases, the students built on these early studies and moved into the more complex issues of group cohesion and conflict.

Example 3: A Children's Self-Healing Program

Our third example is from the work of practitioners in the field, and so needs more details. The example is from work done at the Center for Grieving Children. The Center is a non-profit organization committed to offering a safe environment for children, teens, and adults to express and heal their grief through peer support groups and outreach programs. Many of the children arrive from war torn countries, with their families in the US as refugees.

The Center serves children, teens, families, schools, and communities who are grieving the death of a family member, or coping with the life-threatening illness of a family member or friend. Often, refugees have experienced violence and detention, war trauma, loss of home and family, uncertainty about asylum, poor social conditions, multiple deprivations, and loss of cultural identity. These psychosocial conditions become imperatives in seeking to work with these families and their children.

The basic principles of the program are based on a peer support model. The guiding principles of the Center program are:

1. Grieving is a natural response to change, loss, and the death of a loved one;
2. Grief is individual and has its own time and duration;
3. Within each individual, child or adult, is the natural ability to heal oneself;
4. Caring and acceptance assist in the healing process.

The Center recognizes that their membership is involved in adjusting to the new culture while still suffering from past losses and trauma . Discovering safety within a group of peers can become a gateway for unleashing diffuse feelings, perceptions, and experiences. The group work program at the Center utilizes art and body centred physical activities through which complex feelings and thoughts can be expressed through stories, images and activities.

Figure 3. Self expression through puppetry

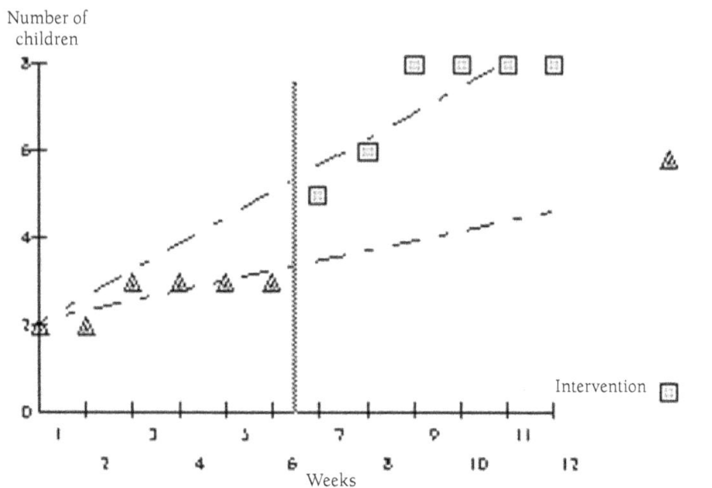

The practice example

In the Baseline Period (Weeks 1-6), a group of eight children were given crayons, paints, clay, and puppet-making material and were encouraged to draw, paint, use clay, and make puppets without pressure or directives from the group worker. For most children, puppetry becomes a very important, emotionally-laden medium.

Intervention Period:(Weeks 7-12)

Beginning at week seven, the children were encouraged to use puppetry to talk about what they had experienced - being abused, mistreated, neglected, victimized, and in some cases, bearing witness to torture and killings. This was, as expected, an upsetting period for the children.

The Intervention in this study was asking the children to create personal puppets that represented power in the natural or imaginative world. That activity; i.e., the Intervention Period, began in session 7 and continued until session 12.

A remarkable series of creative puppets were developed . These included. bees, butterflies, bears, and flowers. Super heroes and heroines emerged as the youngsters drew and decorated their power symbols. Some sub-groups were formed. Children utilized puppets to express personal need and to reach out to other puppets. Themes of caring, friendship, support and concern emerged as the children felt safe enough to ask each other for help. For example, some of the children talked, through their puppets, about what it was like to move from war torn countries, trying to conform to new rules, and different and sometimes strange cultural values. Puppet to puppet, the shared feelings about their difference from other children, how they stood out in the community, and their fear of being beaten up, or attacked - all emerged quite naturally.

In time, some of the children became assertive enough to tell other group members that they did not wish to play in rough physical games.

In Figure 3 above we see the increase in the number of children who created personal puppets which became a vehicle for self-expression.

The triangles show the rate of increase of Self-Expression Through Puppetry in the Baseline Period and its projection into the Intervention Period; that is, the direction that would have been expected if there had been no Intervention during that time.

The boxes show what happened after the Intervention was introduced in session 7. The Intervention mean of 7.17 is more than twice as large, or more than a 200% increase compared to the Baseline mean score of 2.67.

This is another example of how SSD can be used to conduct a group work study and demonstrate the impact of the intervention. This particular study was used with administration and board members to document the effectiveness of the program.

These are merely three examples. Perhaps it is important to note that SSD has been applied to many other problems.

Diversity of SSD groupwork applications

A wide diversity of SSD studies of groupwork is available. Here is a sample of different SSD studies of groupwork:

- Terminal cancer patients (Allison & Rodway, 1983);
- Family therapy (Bentley, 1990);
- Child therapy, (Franklin et al. 2001);
- Institutionalized elderly (Blackman, Pinkston, 1976);
- Southeast Asian Refugees, (Cheung & Canda, 1992);
- Delinquent youth, (Kolko & Milan, 1983);
- Chemically dependent women (Marr & Fairchild, 1993);
- AIDS (Orgnero & Rodway, 1991);
- Battered women (Rubin, 1991).

We are encouraged by the range and variety of these studies, which affords the recognition that groupworkers can utilize this methodology in their respective area of interest. It may help to know a little about the history of developing this method.

Single System Design (SSD): A historical perspective

In the history of social work research in the United States, there is ongoing interest in practitioners conducting research on their own practice. Mary Richmond (1917), regarded by many as the founder of social work in the United States, wrote, 'The practitioner of an art must discover the heart of the whole matter for himself' (p.103). One of the major recommendations of the Milford conference of 1929 was the

> urgent call for increased research activity, especially, the creation of a cadre of practitioner-researchers who understand both practice and research. (Briar, 1972, p.12)

The first SSD textbook was published in 1979 by Jayaratne and Levy. Three critical components of SSD were identified:

1. 'The clinician-researcher must have a thorough understanding of the treatment methods being employed' (p.9). In SSD, specifying the treatment variable(s) permits ongoing measurement and monitoring of the relationship between the intervention(s) and outcome(s).
2. 'The clinician-researcher must have an empirical orientation toward the process of intervention' (p.10). In SSD, variables are converted into measurable attributes which permit the collection of data relevant to the intervention(s) of the practitioner.
3. 'The clinician-researcher must have the ability to functionally use empirical feedback that is obtained during intervention' (p.12). SSD promotes ongoing collection of data generated by the interaction of practitioner and client/group.

The book: *Evaluating Practice: Guidelines for the Accountable Professional* (Bloom & Fischer), first published in 1982, is the classic SSD text in social work. The 1999 edition. (Bloom, Fischer & Orme) includes SINGWIN, an SSD computer program specially designed and created by Dr. Charles Auerbach.

The objective of SSD, according to the authors of *Evaluating Practice* is to provide 'practitioners with the knowledge, skills, and specific procedures to evaluate their own practice' (p.2). The book defines SSD as a 'set of empirical procedures used to observe changes in an identified target (a specified problem or objective of the client) that is measured repeatedly over time.' (Bloom et al. 1999, p.5). In less technical terms, SSD is a method of evaluating changes in one's practice by repeating the same questions over time.

In 1988, the American Council on Social Work Education published the following accreditation standard: ' The content of research should impart scientific methods of building knowledge for practice and of evaluating service delivery in all areas of practice ... The professional foundation content of research should thus provide skills that will take students beyond the role of consumers of research and prepare them to evaluate their own practice systematically' (CSWE, 1988, p.127). That statement became the sanction for teaching SSD in graduate and undergraduate schools of social work in the United States. In this sense, SSD is a relatively new research methodology in social work education.

Finally - why do we think that SSD is helpful to groupwork practitioners? In the next section, we present some of the advantages.

Advantages of the SSD for groupwork research

We believe that Single System Design (SSD), is particularly adapted to group work research for the following reasons:

1. In SSD, the researcher and the practitioner are the same person. As a result, the practice problem investigated will be the practice problem of concern to both the practitioner and researcher.
2. Students conducting SSD research are in fact studying their own practice. Typical responses are, 'It didn't feel as if I was doing research ... I was able to look and see what was and was not working ... I was able to share the information with my clients, They really liked the graphs ... I was able to demonstrate my work to my supervisor.' Dr. Ivanoff, of Columbia University School of Social Work, described her experience with students in her SSD research class in these words: 'They (the students) have become better able to identify specific problems, goals and intervention, and their inferential thinking is challenged' (Ivanoff, 1990, p.63). In a 1996 study of 136 graduate students at the Wurzweiler School of Social Work, 'More than 95% of the students surveyed found the program added a .... valuable component to research, and 81.9% reported the program helpful in evaluating practice' (Conboy et al. 1996, p. 127).
3. Practice-evaluation in SSD includes visual analysis, as well as statistical analysis ranging from simple descriptive statistics to interpretative statistics. Examples of the former will be offered later.
4. Studies conducted by uninvolved researchers are much more likely to

present data on individual members, than on the group as a whole. SSD provides the practitioner with information about the group-as-a-whole, as well as individuals in the group.

5. The language of intervention in SSD is not an abstraction, but a description of specific interventions, by the practitioner, as they emerge in practice.
6. SSD is theory-free. The method can be used with any theoretical orientation. Where indicated, modified or a different theoretical orientation may be introduced into each practice situation.
7. By definition and structure, SSD is a practice-based evaluation methodology and fits in very nicely with the *American Standards for Social Work Practice with Groups*: 'Monitoring and evaluation of success of groups in accomplishing its objectives through observation and measurement of outcomes and/or processes.' (AASWG, 1998, p.3).

Conclusion

The call for social work practitioners to conduct their own research is almost 90 years old (Richmond, 1917). It took more than 60 years before the first SSD social work text was published (Jayarante & Levy, 1979). The classic *Evaluating Practice* (Bloom & Fischer), was published in 1982. The 1999 edition of *Evaluating Practice* includes a SSD computer program designed by Dr. Charles Auerbach. SSD became a required research course in undergraduate and graduate schools of social work in the United States in 1984. In this sense, SSD is regarded as a relatively new research methodology.

SSD has some unique features. The most obvious one is that the practitioner and the researcher are the same person. There are at least two consequences. One is the likelihood that the problem selected for research is the problem of greatest concern to the practitioner. The second is a heightened sense of interest in and commitment to research as a tool to enhance practice effectiveness. It is difficult to talk about a research-practice gap, or conflict between researchers and practitioners, when the researcher and the practitioner are the same person.

Fritz Redl, a leading social work researcher in the 1950s wrote:

> The practitioner has an odd complaint. He politely admits that the research expert produces a lot that is important. His complaint is that the research expert does not answer the questions he asks. (Reddl, 1950, p.16)

In SSD, the practitioners, based on his/her practice situation, in consultation with the client, formulates the research questions to be asked.

In *Evaluating Practice,* (Bloom et al, 1999), the authors highlight the importance of Visual Analysis. They write:

> Probably the most basic analytic method of single-system designs is ... a visual analysis-a comparison of the data ... during the intervention phase with the data you collected during the baseline periods. (p.513)

An examination of the three graphs we presented suggest the effectiveness of the respective group programs. However, these are not merely academic exercises. As noted by one of the students above, 'I was able to share the information with my clients. They really liked the graphs'.

Groupwork researchers have identified a number of challenging problems involved in conducting group work studies (Brower & Rose, 1989). One is the limited external validity of group work studies, i.e., the ability to generalize beyond the group which is being studied.

We approach this issue as practitioners who routinely deal with this problem by utilizing general group work practice principles. Given that practitioners are able to generalize from one group to another, SSD methodology which is shaped and influenced by practice principles, can be useful in monitoring and studying this process. Once effectiveness has been demonstrated, opportunities to compare similar groups can and should be undertaken. SSD, it should be noted, has the capacity to study and compare multiple groups.

A second issue involved in studying group work practice is accounting for the differential responses of group members to the same stimuli. How do practitioners deal with this issue? The skilled groupwork practitioner treats differential responses to the same stimuli as a normal group behavior. For the practitioner, the point is to harness these differences, which in many cases determine the success or failure of the group. SSD is particularly adapted to monitoring this process, highlighting critical factors which help to shape and influence the group process as it unfolds.

A third issue raised by group work researchers involves accounting for uncontrolled variables - those issues that are not directly observed and monitored; for example, who attends which session or age differences that were not considered important at first. These variables may be regarded by the uninvolved groupwork researcher as uncontrolled variables. Yet, for practitioners, these aspects are critical variables which influence group process. In SSD, these factors are often central to the development of the group, and can be made part of the research later - when new aspects are noticed. In sum, everything important to practice is important to SSD.

Over time, we reviewed a series of SSD studies of groupwork conducted by groupworkers and researchers. Whereas groupworkers using SSD tended to present group data, uninvolved researchers are much likely to present data on individual group members. This difference suggests the value of SSD studies conducted by groupworkers.

Since the inception of social work, it has taken more than a hundred years to develop a research methodology aimed at practitioners. SSD research methodology is user-friendly to practitioners. We look forward to this new partnership between SSD and group work practitioners which has the potential to benefit individuals, groups, organizations, neighborhoods and communities.

References

AASWG (1998) *Standards for Social Work Practice with Groups*. Item IJ. Akron, OH: Association for the Advancement of Social Work with Groups

Allison, H., Gripton, J. and Rodway, M. (1983) Social work services as a component of palliative care with terminal cancer patients. *Social Work in Health Care*, 8, 4, 29-44

Bentley, K.J. (1990) An evaluation of family-based intervention using single-system research. *British Journal of Social Work*, 20, 101-116

Blackman, D.K., Howe, M. and Pinkston, E.M. (1976) Increasing participation in social interaction of the institutionalized elderly. *Gerontologist*, 16, 12, 69-76

Bloom, M., Fischer, J. and Orme, J. (1999) *Evaluating Practice: Guidelines for the Accountable Professional*. (3rd Edition). Boston: Allan & Bacon

Briar, S. (1974) *Social Casework: Generic and specific*. (A Report of the Milford Conference, 1929). Washington, DC: National Association of Social Workers

Cheung, K.F.M. & Canda, E.R. (1992) Training Southeast Asian refugees as social workers: A single subject evaluation. *Social Development Issues*, 14, 2/3, 88-99

Conboy, A., Auerbach, C., Beckerman, A., Schnall, D. and LaPorte, H.H. (2000) *Research on Social Work Practice*, 10, 1, 127-138

CSWE (1988) *Curriculum Policy Statement*. Section, 6.13. Washington, DC: Council on Social Work Education

Franklin, C., Biever, J., Moore, K., Clemons, D. and Scamardo, M. (2001) The Effectiveness of Solution-Focused Therapy with Children in a School Setting. *Research on Social Work Practice*, 11, 4, 411-435

Ivanoff, L. (1990). Research utilization: Reflections on the rhetoric. in L. Videka-Sherman and W.J. Reid (Eds.) *Advances in Clinical Social Work Research.* Silver Spring, MD: NASW Press

Jayaratne, S. and Levy, L. (1979) *Empirical Clinical Practice.* New York: Columbia University Press

Kolko, D.K. and Milan, M.A. (1983) Reframing and paradoxical instruction to overcome resistance in the treatment of delinquent youths: A multiple baseline analysis. *Journal of Consulting and Clinical Psychology*, 51, 655-660

Marr, D.D. and Fairchild, T.N. (1993). A problem-solving strategy and self-esteem in recovering chemically dependent women. *Alcoholism Treatment Quarterly*, 10, 1/2, 171-186

Orgnero, M.I. and Rodway, M.R. (1991). AIDS and social work treatment: A single-system analysis. *Health and Social Work*, 16, 2, 123-141

Richmond, M. (1917). *Social Diagnosis.* New York: Russell Sage

Rubin, A. (1991). The effectiveness of outreach counseling and support groups for battered women: A preliminary evaluation. *Research on Social Work Practice*, 1, 4, 332-357

Schwartz, W. (1961) The Social Worker in the Group. in *New Perspectives on Services to Groups: Theory, organization, practice.* New York: National Association of Social Workers

This chapter was first published in 2001 in *Groupwork* Vol. 13(1), pp.57-72

At the time of writing, Paul Johnson, was Assistant Professor, Dept of Social Work, University of Southern Maine, Aaron Beckerman was Professor Emeritus, Wurzweiler School of Social Work, Yeshiva University, New York, and Charles Auerbach was Professor, Wurzweiler School of Social Work, Yeshiva University, New York

www.ingramcontent.com/pod-product-compliance
Lightning Source LLC
Chambersburg PA
CBHW061737270326
41928CB00011B/2266

* 9 7 8 1 8 6 1 7 7 1 0 7 0 *